FAITH WITHOUT DOGMA

By the same author
THE ROOT OF THE MATTER

Faith Without Dogma

IN QUEST OF MEANING

BY

MARGARET ISHERWOOD

HARPER & ROW, PUBLISHERS
NEW YORK AND EVANSTON

TO

BEN, ANNE AND LIN

I am the slave of the spirit of the quest
KABIR

ACKNOWLEDGEMENTS

My thanks are due to all authors and publishers who have kindly given permission for the inclusion of copyright material in this book; to the specialists who read parts of the manuscript, especially Sir Julian and Lady Huxley, Dr Martin Davidson, F.R.A.S., and Professor Alec Mace; to the children who unknowingly provided the material for the chapters on Education, and above all to Dorothy and Leonard Elmhirst whose unfailing help and inspiration have made the book possible.

FOREWORD

This book is intended only for seekers in quest of meaning; it is not for those who feel they already know all the answers. The life of Dag Hammerskjold was said to have been a constant search for meaning, and this is true of all reflective minds that need a deeper and more comprehensive understanding of life than that proffered by orthodox Christianity, or any other credal religion.

Throughout the ages the hunger for meaning has stirred the imaginations of men to create some explanation of what life is all about, of how it began and the nature of its purpose, if any. There has generally been unquestioning acquiescence in these 'explanations' until contact with another tribal culture and/or the development of analytic thought has thrown doubt on their truth.

Today it is increasingly felt that a world religion is needed and that it should be built, not on authoritarian pronouncements, but on the basis of objectively established fact on the one hand, and on subjective spiritual experience on the other.

It is the claim of this book that adequate grounds for such a scientifically based religious faith can be found in these two realms. It is true that for the present we must, as Paul said, be content with partial knowledge, with seeing only puzzling reflections in a mirror. Yet the fact is that we have in the story of evolution that science has unfolded, indications of a trend towards ever-increasing significance; and in the mind of man, in spite of all that is evil and immature, we have a trend towards the expansion of consciousness and the deepening of his capacity for experiencing and implementing spiritual values.

In these two areas of the inner and outer, it is possible to find life meaningful in a much more comprehensive and less controversial sense than that of narrow doctrinal creeds—but only if we are prepared to do the work involved. Therefore I would say with Jacob Boehme: 'If you are not a self-transformer, let my book alone'.

M.I.

CONTENTS

FOREWORD
   I *The Pathway to Meaning*   *page* 15

THE EVOLUTION OF CONSCIOUSNESS
  II *Self-Ignorance*   30
 III *Self-Knowledge Through Self-Observation*   38
 IV *The True Self*   47
  V *Cosmic Consciousness*   54
 VI *Symbolism in Religious Thinking*   63
 VII *Paranormal Consciousness*   77

THE EVOLUTION OF LIFE
 VIII *Cosmogenesis*   86
 IX *Biogenesis and Noogenesis*   92
  X *The Challenge of Life*   103
APPENDIX I *Emotional and Social Aspects*   107
APPENDIX II *Intellectual Aspects*   113

CHAPTER I

The Pathway to Meaning

> *Mankind stands accused of arrested development. To try to go back to the imagined simplicities of the past is impossible. To try to stand still in the midst of the present perplexities . . . is to court disaster. To try to cross new frontiers of the mind and spirit seems to be the only truly live option.*
>
> FLOYD ROSS: *Man, Myth and Maturity*[1]

In this frightening yet stimulating moment of world history, we are confronted with two burning problems which are intimately related: how to build a viable society which will include all men, and how to find meaning which will take us beyond the life we know and enable us to see both life and death as transitional aspects of one single significant process. Nothing less will satisfy man's deepest need and make it possible for him to live well and wisely during his brief stay on this planet.

The problem of meaning is a relatively new one for the Western world. Before the rise of modern science man's belief in an anthropomorphic God who had created him and placed him in a favourable position at the centre of a secure and static universe gave a perfectly adequate explanation of existence. Now modern psychology disturbs him with the suggestion that such an image of God is but the projection of his own unconscious imaginings, and modern astronomy tells him that he is not the centre of a cozy cosmos designed for his especial benefit, but that his planet is but an infinitesimal part of an expanding universe, one of millions of other planets, some of which may be inhabited by beings superior to himself. Clearly our childish concepts will have to go and our religious thinking be revised if it is to cohere with scientific discovery.

[1] Minns Lectures, Boston, 1958, p. 56.

Religion and science can no longer be kept in watertight com-
partments for neither can be in a healthy condition in isolation
from the other. In times past religion attempted from motives of
fear to suppress scientific thinking. 'Man's presumptuous brain'
has retaliated to that suppression not only by undermining some
of the beliefs that religion was trying to preserve, but, far more
serious, by going ahead faster than the growth of those spiritual
qualities that religion was trying to foster—such qualities as
tenderness, insight, sensitivity and understanding. The result is a
world teetering on the brink of self-destruction, for the qualities
mentioned form the cement which holds society together.

To redress the balance we must now start at a new place and
instead of asking 'what am I to believe?' ask 'How can I get a
clearer knowledge and understanding of myself?' For the self—
the total self and not just the intellect—is the instrument through
which we win knowledge of truth, and if it is malformed or
dissociated at any of its levels—as is the case in some degree with
everyone—our knowledge of truth will suffer accordingly.

Man is an altogether new kind of animal from any that has
preceded him in the long life journey and he must now face the
necessity of undertaking an altogether new kind of evolution, the
evolution of mind. Unless he can do this he will lose his *raison
d'être* as a species. The important thing about man therefore is
not the rather sorry creature which, despite Hamlet's eulogy,[1] he
now is, but what he may become. There is no reason to suppose
that in the millenia ahead his advance may not be as stupendous
as that of the unicellular organism to *homo sapiens*, provided
only that he takes his development seriously. Having achieved
consciousness and self-consciousness, together with what seems
like a modest power of choice, further progress will depend upon
his willingness to grow and to pay the price of growth.

This means amongst other things willingness to relinquish
static concepts that have served their turn and to move imagina-
tively into new areas of thought, discarding nothing of authentic
value, but daring to envisage wider horizons in our religious
thinking as we have done in our scientific thinking. There is firm
ground for faith in life in the story of man's remarkable journey

[1] 'What a piece of work is a man! How noble in reason! How infinite
in faculties! in form and moving, how express and admirable! in action,
how like an angel! in apprehension, how like a god! the beauty of the
world! the paragon of animals.' *Hamlet*. Act II, Scene 2.

from the mud, and there is inspiration in the thought that he is not at the end of that journey—or need not be. The choice before us is momentous.

When disaster overtakes us in the external world it is always followed by most careful investigation and no effort is spared until a cause, such as metal fatigue in the Comet aeroplanes, has been diagnosed. But when the cause of disaster lies not in things external but in ourselves, in our uneducated and uncontrolled emotions, then mental rather than metal fatigue has set in. Inertia and fear keep us from making the necessary research which would require change in ourselves. This is partly because it is far more difficult to explore personality than to explore the complex mechanism of an aeroplane. 'Know thyself' sounds a simple enough directive, but in fact we have few techniques for achieving this kind of 'inside information', for being at once subject and object, observer and observed, and for seeing ourselves not only 'as others see us', which may or may not be an accurate picture, but as we really are in contrast to what we like to think we are.

In the second place we are afraid of what we might find if we looked honestly into ourselves and faced our true motives. It is therefore simpler to build a socially acceptable mask behind which to hide and to rationalize our self-deception with the cliché that introspection is morbid, that 'a moral nation does not need such men; that sane, clean-living folk do not concern themselves with what may or may not go on inside their heads'.[1]

Quite apart from the fact that this is bad mental hygiene for the individual, it is extremely dangerous for the race, as the dreadful history of this century has demonstrated. For over fifty years now we have been warned that instinctive forces do not remain inactive because we remain unaware of them, that unless we can integrate these forces with our conscious thinking, sooner or later they will find a way of breaking through the habitual controls and will submerge us.

Whatever has not been resolved within the psyche will eventually express itself in our external lives and will determine our fate. If therefore the catastrophes that overtake man have their origin in his unconscious mind, it is only common sense to take the understanding of the psyche as the most serious of all tasks.

[1] From a contemporary letter in the *Daily Express* on the subject of depth psychologists.

If the individual cannot achieve regeneration, there is no hope for society which is composed of individuals. No sort of mass movement, not even a 'religious' revival, will do the work which has to be done by each human being on himself. It is certainly our bounden duty to strive for greater social justice and to improve the economic structure of the countries of the world. But to leave the main instrument of improvement unchanged is to leave ourselves wide open to invasion both from the greed, hate, jealousy and fear in our own natures and from the persuasiveness of any chance power-lover.

The Church,[1] whose primary concern is said to be with man's regeneration, should help us here. But the Church is under heavy criticism at the present time because, instead of emphasizing the necessity of inner growth through self-knowledge and self-transformation, it teaches static doctrines 'once and for all delivered' as the way to salvation. Some wit has written:

> 'Like a mighty tortoise moves the Church of God;
> Brothers' we are treading where we've always trod.'[2]

There is truth in the couplet but, to be fair, only a half truth. The Church at its best is moving forward[3] and striving to hold men to their own highest standards. There are liberal thinkers among all groups who do not take their stand on inert and static doctrines, who do not discourage independent thinking and who do not themselves believe in a God who, affronted by man's wickedness, required atonement to be made in the torture and death of his 'Only Son'. Pastors of psychological insight know that Christ died because we are the kind of people we are—power-loving, cruel, unimaginative and barely conscious of what we do; that he did not die 'to pay the price of sin' or

> 'That we might go at last to Heaven,
> Saved by his precious blood.'

as the still universally popular hymn teaches.

[1] 'The Church' in this book should be understood as referring to any and every branch of the Christian Church, and to its members as well as its administrators.
[2] *The Christian Century*: an Ecumenical Weekly. Established 1884. Named Xth Century 1900. 407 S. Dearborn Street, Chicago 5, Ill., USA.
[3] The psychologist Dr Cyril Burt writes: 'The more scholarly of the professional clergy of every denomination are inclining more and more to a more flexible way of thought'. This fact is illustrated in frequent discussions on the air and in much current religious writing.

Yet in spite of the fact that the Church at its best is neither literalist, bigoted or intolerant, it must be admitted that, taken as a whole, it shows but little interest in the one thing needful, the development and transforming of the human mind; that it stresses the importance of doctrinal belief more than increase in wisdom and understanding; and that it fails to build adequate bridges whereby the individual may pass from either a barren agnosticism on the one hand or a narrow-minded sectarianism on the other, to faith in life itself and to a sense of responsibility for helping to further life's highest purposes.

It is surely an astonishing thing that, after nearly two thousand years of Christian teaching and preaching, the Church does not initiate research into the problem of why crime and mental disorders are on the increase and war remains an ever more menacing possibility; that it does not ask wherein its own shortcomings may lie, and what might be done to minimize them over and above putting on the same ineffective record. The old story of Salvation still brings comfort and a sense of security to many, and how many yearn for these things is evident in the numerous hymns such as:

> 'Rock of Ages, cleft for me,
> Let me hide myself in Thee.'

But this will no longer do. In the precarious society we have created there is 'no place to hide' or to indulge our infantile longings. Moreover we are part of a universe which is in its entirety one vast process of becoming and therefore we also must become. We may stand still on a moving staircase but not in living. There our 'salvation', in every sense of the word, depends on moving forward across 'new frontiers of mind and spirit', on relinquishing both the security of the nursery and the habits of the jungle.

Dr Edward Glover writes that 'The absence of serious research into the nature of war constitutes one of the most amazing blindspots in the history of human endeavour'.[1] Research into the causes of war means research into the nature of man who makes war, and this is a task for the church as well as for the psychologist, for the concern of the church is also with the regeneration of man. Not that such research will bring any quick and clear solutions to man's fearful predicament, but a change of attitude

[1] Edward Glover, 'Is Change Progress?', The Listener, December 5, 1963.

can of itself be revolutionary. One such necessary change is in our protopathic[1] or indiscriminate way of feeling and thinking. We like things to be clear-cut, black or white, good or evil, so that 'we know where we are' and feel secure accordingly. In the lessons published by the Catholic Enquiry Centre, it is asserted that 'Only the Catholic Church knows its own mind'.[2] But it is sometimes a mark of maturity not to know one's own mind, and to be able to retain an attitude of suspended judgment about matters on which equally wise men hold different opinions. To be capable of enduring uncertainty is not to be guilty of 'floosy thinking'; it is rather to show a capacity for discriminate and careful thinking.

In this century we have learned that security in personal relations is absolutely essential to the emotional health of the small child, but as we grow towards maturity we have to understand something which has been called 'The Wisdom of Insecurity'[3] and to learn that faith is not won by clinging to the thought-patterns of the past but by seeking their deeper meaning. Our business is growth and no growth can take place where everything is certain, static and secure. To crave the security of changelessness is like trying to hold running water in one's hand. We have therefore to learn how to loosen our grasp,

> 'To take by leaving,
> To hold by letting go.'[4]

It is a matter of great encouragement that a marked 'wind of change' is now blowing from a quarter which has seemed for long to make a virtue of changelessness, that is from within the Vatican itself. The late Pope John pleaded for a drawing together in mutual understanding, not only between all Christians, but between all men 'who are endowed with the light of reason and a natural and operative honesty'. Still more recently Pope Paul, at the General Council of the Church of Rome in November 1963, showed quite startling courage in denouncing the Holy Office as 'a stumbling-block and a scandal', and said that 'other Churches have much to teach the Roman Church, and that they too are vehicles of God's grace'. This is surely tantamount to admitting the right of religious liberty to all. It is definitely out of harmony

[1] The terms 'protopathic' and 'epicritic' were coined by Dr Rivers, F.R.S., to distinguish 'All-or-none' from more discriminating reactions.
[2] Catholic Enquiry Centre, 120 West Heath Road, London N.W.3.
[3] Alan Watts, *The Wisdom of Insecurity*. New York, Pantheon, 1951.
[4] Edward Carpenter, *Towards Democracy*. London, Allen & Unwin, 1883.

with the claim that the Roman Church is 'the one chosen vessel of God's truth'[1] or that 'God founded the Catholic Church to speak on His behalf' and that therefore, for a Catholic, 'it would be disloyalty to God to enter any other'.[2]

If the Papacy itself continues to disparage such inflexibility we may dare to hope that the World Council of Churches will soon reach the conclusion that superficial differences between Christians are irrelevant compared with the love of truth and good, and that it will then become interested in seeking for the common ground which should unite all great religions. The present attitude which maintains that unity with Buddhism is impossible because 'Buddhism does not even believe in God'[3] is a provincial attitude, concerned more with uniformity of belief under the aegis of 'my church' than with that 'unity of the spirit which is the bond of peace'. The Spirit bloweth where it listeth' even into the realm of non-Christian religions; indeed it is sometimes more in evidence there. It is arrogant of Christians to claim a monopoly of the presence of God the Holy Ghost.

'The letter killeth; the spirit giveth life.' This is just as true when the 'letter' of religious doctrine is allowed to form barriers between people as when 'iron curtains' are hung between those of one social ideology and another. Nicolas Berdyaev writes that 'The religion of the Spirit will be the religion of man when he has come of age' and nearly a thousand years ago Abelard said 'The religion of the Father and the Son is ended; the religion of the Spirit is begun'. It is begun, but it is taking us a very long time to 'come of age'. What does the phrase mean? Perhaps it means awakening to the realization that 'there are not three Gods but one God',[4] an all-pervading Spirit. In this case to be 'of age' would mean to be primarily concerned with the things of the Spirit, not with the divisive creeds and sects, and it would mean being able to share our thoughts and experiences about spiritual things with those who differ from us at the surface level.

When the Buddhist U Thant received word that his son had been killed, he asked for two hours alone. During that period he attained the courage and calm to enable him to return quietly to his work. How could he have done this save through contact with

[1] Words of Dr. Heenan quoted in the *Observer*, December 31, 1961.
[2] Lessons published by the Catholic Enquiry Centre. *Op. cit.*
[3] An Anglican viewpoint, expressed on the BBC.
[4] See 'The Athanasian Creed'. *The Book of Common Prayer.*

the spirit dwelling within him? Therefore in reply to the indictment that Buddhists do not believe in God, the question must be asked: 'In which God do Buddhists not believe?' A member of the Society of Friends has defined atheism as 'disbelief in the God of someone else', a perceptive statement which makes atheists of many 'believers'. However we interpret the biblical declaration that 'God created man in His own image' (an assertion which only makes sense if taken to mean that a spark of the divine exists potentially in all men), man has certainly reversed the process and made his God in accordance with his own nature and his own emotional needs. For a warm outgoing disposition, as well as for one who has been starved of love, 'God' will probably be envisaged as a loving father-figure; for another, tormented by unresolved hate and aggression, He will be more like a punitive sovereign judge, ready to destroy any who disobey or disagree; for the authoritarian temperament, He will be a not-very-benevolent-despot who does not tolerate freedom of thought and 'saves' only the submissive. For mature individuals, capable of some degree of abstract thought, He will be the unknown source of all values, the ground of all being, the all-pervading creative spirit of life.

Since then our God tends to be conceived as the apotheosis of our values and our emotional needs, clearly what is important is not our particular religious labels or beliefs, but the nature of our values, the quality of our living, and the depth of our understanding. What we know of God as 'Reality' will be proportionate to what we know of these. All can at least agree with Blake that

> 'Where mercy, truth and pity dwell,
> There God is dwelling too' [1]

no matter what a man's race or creed, or lack of creed.

Meister Eckhart, a very mature Christian of the thirteenth century, advised his congregation not to 'prate' too much about God, as if they knew who and what and where He was. Gautama shared this attitude and taught men to concentrate on growth towards the Light until they could know It within themselves, rather than on arguing Its existence or worshipping those in whom they saw Its presence. He once said 'It is not necessary to worship a Buddha; it is necessary to become a buddha. I claim to have seen the light. I see things in reality. But please do not

---

[1] William Blake's poem 'To Mercy, Pity, Peace and Love'.

accept my teaching because I say so; do not accept it unless it is in accord with your own reasoning.'

The light seen by the Buddha, the Illumined One, and by the Christ, the Anointed One, was the same light. They were on the same spiritual wavelength and therefore their teaching was essentially the same teaching. They might reasonably be regarded as belonging to a new order of men, the pioneers of a new humanity. The disclaimer of Jesus to perfection in the words : 'Why callest thou me good? There is none good but one; that is God',[1] suggests that, no more than Gautama, did he desire to be worshipped. His surprising directive 'Be ye perfect'[2] indicates that the way into the new Life of which he spoke is the difficult way of transforming of self rather than the easy way of deification of another. 'Why call ye me Lord, Lord, and do not the things which I say?'[3]

When the teaching of the masters is taken seriously, the confused tangle of life's problems will begin to loosen; so also will the religious problems of the doubter. For the teaching does not ask him to begin his search for meaning by believing certain debatable doctrines, but to think for himself and to work at the very exacting task of increasing self-awareness and insight. It thus spares him the agonizing choice between abandoning his intellectual integrity by remaining securely in the fold, or living as a disillusioned 'outsider' who can find no meaning in life. Such a dilemma is based on false alternatives. The real existential alternatives are not between belief and doubt but between the way of life and growth and the way of despair and spiritual death; between adopting the attitude of the research scientist who knows that all his findings are but a pebble on the great shore of truth, and the blind arrogance of the bigot who 'knows' that, as the Rishis put it, 'he has the whole ocean ladled into his own little pond'.

The individual, brought up in a narrow church which mistakes instruction for education, is in grave danger should he ever begin to think for himself and to question authority of church or book; not, we hope, in danger of physical persecution[4] but of mental or

[1] St Matthew xix, 17.
[2] St Matthew v, 48
[3] St Luke vi, 46.
[4] But that the danger of religious persecution is not over can be seen in Monsignor Knox's book *The Belief of Catholics*, London, Sheed & Ward, 1953, which claims that a Catholic government would have the right to 'deport or imprison those who unsettled the minds of its subjects with new doctrines'.

spiritual collapse. The form breakdown takes in any one person will vary according to temperament. At worst he may drift into a totally materialistic attitude which argues that, since nothing can be known, nothing matters; one may as well get all the enjoyment one can out of life while the going's good. Where spiritual good and ethical values have been made to appear dependent on a creed (as in Paul's assertion, 'If Christ is not raised, then our gospel is null and void and so is your faith'),[1] loss of belief in that creed may result in loss of all interest in the spiritual values which have been associated with it. When these values have never been experienced as valid in their own right, they may go out with the 'bath water'; the 'heavenly treasure' may lose all significance along with the 'earthen vessel' that contained it. This attitude is a fruitful source of crime, both juvenile and adult.

Mature and sensitive temperaments will suffer more deeply and sink, not into materialism but into an unhappy agnosticism or, if utterly overwhelmed by the horror and cruelty of life, into a nihilism which asserts:

> 'The look of all the world's a lie, a face made up
> O'er graves and fiery depths; and nothing's true
> But what is horrible.'[2]

They may come to agree with the final word of H. G. Wells on what, at the end of his life, he referred to as 'this doomed formicary. Our world of self-delusion . . . will perish amidst its evasions and fatuities. It is like a convoy lost in darkness on an unknown rocky coast, with quarrelling pirates in the chart-room and savages clambering up the sides of the ships to plunder and do evil as the whim may take them. That is the rough outline of the more and more jumbled movie on the screen before us. Mind near exhaustion still makes its final futile movement towards that "way out or round or through the impasse". . . . There is no way out or round or through. . . . There is no "Pattern of Things to Come". . . . *Homo sapiens*, as he has been pleased to call himself, is in his present form played out.'[3]

Suicide may be, and sometimes has been, the outcome of such a conclusion. We have heard much about the emotionally damag-

---

[1] I Corinthians xv, 14.
[2] Beddoes, *Death's Jest Book*.
[3] H. G. Wells, *Mind at the End of its Tether*, p. 15. Heinemann.

ing effects of traumatic experiences in early life, but no study has yet been made of the effect on sensitive natures of the trauma caused by the loss of a faith which once gave life meaning. The loss can of course be just as devastating if the faith was a 'secular' one. When Douglas Hyde, erstwhile News Editor of the *Daily Worker*, asked a Communist friend why, since she was in such disagreement with the Party's aims and policies, she did not resign, he received the reply: 'I will do it if you think I ought. But don't hold me responsible for what happens next, because I may do what poor old Jan Masaryk has just done. You see I'm terrified of the vacuum that would be left in my life if I went.'[1]

If Masaryk did in fact commit suicide it was not for this reason, but the point of the story is that the loss of what has hitherto given life meaning can be almost or quite unbearable. Those who find themselves able to struggle on may look around at other 'isms' and ideologies, hoping to find one which can fill the empty place. But having once been 'duped', they will tread rather sceptically and may, at the end of the survey, say with Browning:

'We all surmise, They, this thing, and I, that:
Whom shall my soul believe?'[2]

The fact is that the thoughtful seeker can never again take over and believe in someone else's system of beliefs. It is no good going on a hunting expedition, like Shaw's *Black Girl in Search of God*, in the mistaken idea that somebody, somewhere must have the answer, must have privileged access to 'the' truth. Even psychology, so often turned to for help when theology has failed, may have nothing to tell us. Jung's statement that all his patients who came to him over the age of thirty-five came because they could find no meaning to life is well known. 'It is safe to say that every one of them fell ill because he had lost that which the religions of every age have given to their followers.'[3] No more than anyone else had Jung ready-made answers of the sort they were seeking. 'I had to tell them that the meaning of life could not be bought for a fee', could not be handed in a package over the psychological any more than over the theological counter.

---

[1] Douglas Hyde, *I Believed*, p. 289. Wm. Heinemann.
[2] Robert Browning, 'Rabbi Ben Ezra', Stanza 22.
[1] Jung, *Modern Man in Search of a Soul*, p. 137. Kegan Paul.

Such large questions as the meaning of life, the existence of God, the immortality of the soul are not amenable to the kind of test or proof that the scientist can make about matters of measurable fact. Therefore the only answer the wise guide can give is a question: 'Are you willing to undertake a journey?' and the only advice the wise guide will offer is that made by the Zen Buddhist master to his pupil: 'Walk on'. In other words: do not give up or look back; do not cling nostalgically to the discarded literalisms of childhood's imagery, but seek for the deeper meaning which that imagery symbolized. There is an answer, but not where you are looking. The answer is to be found in following the way of creative inner growth. It cannot be condensed into verbal statements.

Shortly before his death, Jung himself was asked in a BBC interview whether he believed in God. He replied: 'All that I have learned has led me step by step to an unshakeable conviction of the existence of God. I only believe in what I know. Therefore I do not take his existence on belief. I know that he exists.'

Some seekers may feel relieved and reassured by this confession of faith and may argue from it 'Well that's fine; if a great psychologist believed in God, then it's all right for me to believe in him'. But we cannot thus lightly appropriate the religious faith acquired by the effort and experience of another. Certainly we should be wise to give attention to his message that there *is* a vision at the end of the road, but if we want to see it we must make the same 'step by step' journey into life. For religious knowledge is of a different order from factual knowledge. It cannot be handed on; it can only be won.

The only sort of guide who can help the lost seeker is one who has himself made the journey through the dark night of the soul. With conspicuous honesty the late Archbishop Temple, after giving an address to an audience with whom he had failed to make contact, remarked to a friend: 'I couldn't reach them because, you see, I have never doubted'. Throughout life he had found it puzzling that anyone should doubt, so he and his audience were in 'psychological space', unable to meet.

Fortunately a very important event is now in process, a new kind of guide has begun to appear; one who might be called a religious psychologist or a psychological 'religionist', one who knows that the way out is the way up as well as the way in; who recognises that, in addition to the lower unconscious, the level of instinctive passions and of repressed complexes, there is a higher unconscious which is also superconscious and which is the source of spiritual energies, of inspiration in the fields of art, science and all types of genius, as well as of mystic experience, illumination and ecstasy.

Hitherto analytic psychology has been primarily concerned with the instinctive aspect of what is rather vaguely referred to as 'the unconscious'. No more important discovery has ever been made than the laying bare of this hidden aspect of the psyche and the realization that mental health requires its integration with consciousness. But although such integration may save us from neurosis and other forms of mental breakdown, it is not enough. It does not inspire us with the will to live or point the way towards the meaning of life, knowledge of which is also essential to mental health. Self-analysis is certainly necessary to clear the pathway and to discover 'what makes us tick', but for what has it been cleared? Where do we go from here?

We go towards the recognition of the superconscious, the higher unconscious or not-yet-conscious variously called the over-self, true self, the Self, the inner reality, which is a spark of the 'divine' or universal mind. But all these high-sounding phrases are mere words unless we have known their meaning in personal experience. Can we have such knowledge?

A man who had been blinded in middle life was asked by a friend: 'Do you not feel tempted to self-pity and despair?' He admitted the temptation and the regrets that at times assailed him because of all the things he could not now do and the places he would never see. Then he added: 'But I also find in myself something else which says "I can manage, I am equal to this"'.

An Austrian psychiatrist[1] has written of how this 'something else' came alive for him amid the horror of the concentration camp. 'I sensed my spirit piercing through the enveloping gloom. I felt it transcend that hopeless, meaningless world, and from somewhere I heard a victorious "Yes" in answer to my question of the existence of an ultimate purpose.'

In such experiences, psychology and religion are seen to be one. The 'within' meets the 'beyond' and Pascal's words are verified: 'Thou wouldst not seek me if thou hadst not already found me'. In other words one does not seek from a vacuum. This 'something

[1] Viktor Frankl, *From Death-Camp to Existentialism*. Boston, Beacon Press, 1959.

else' is the spark or seed of divine life—in theological terms the God immanent which is already there waiting our discovery of 'Him' or 'It'. It is the upward reach in us which resists the downward pull; it is the 'aspiration for the stars' which directs the mind away from its 'nostalgie pour la boue'; it is the spiritual Self or Centre which has the power, if we have the will, to bring under its control all other aspects of the psyche, thus rescuing man from despair and taking him forward towards new realms of being.

This 'something else' is what Jung was referring to when he said that he had come step by step to knowledge of God. By the term 'God' he did not mean an external, remote, omnipotent being but 'a mighty activity in my soul'. The awakening to the presence of this activity, be it faint or mighty, is the answer to the seeker's quest for meaning, because co-operation with the activity is itself felt as meaningful, as relating us to the whole cosmic process of which we are part.

This is not a new discovery. It has been known to men of religious insight throughout the ages. It is the meaning of the strange Hindu sutra 'Tat tvam asi: thou art That' and of similar mystic sayings such as 'be thou thyself and I will be thine' or 'Be what thou art', what thou potentially art, as the hawthorn seed is potentially a rose. Martin Buber has called it the I-Thou relationship, that is to say the relationship between That which is within and That which lies beyond.

It is also of course the essence of the teaching of the Gospels as expressed in the conversation with Nicodemus, in the parables, and in the Sermon on the Mount. Whatever our Christology, whatever our views as to the metaphysical nature of this Rabbi, Son of God or Son of Man or both, his teaching stands. Each age must express the hidden truth of that teaching in its own idiom and in terms of its own new knowledge. The rediscovery of the spirit in man by holistic depth psychology gives new point to the question: 'What will a man gain by winning the whole world at the cost of his true self?'[1] His true self is that which is potentially divine at the centre of his being, the 'God' immanent.

When this new-old religion is understood as a matter not of believing but of self-transforming, unfolding, learning and becoming, several things begin to happen. The problem of the vacuum will drop away as meaning gradually emerges out of the growth process and we become capable of functioning more

[1] St Mark viii, 36.

effectively in the related spheres of body, mind and spirit. Competition between nations and between religions will also drop away as the 'experiment in depth' replaces the love of power and the desire to triumph over others. The only place for competition left to man will be competition with his self of yesterday.

CHAPTER II

Self-Ignorance

> *To acknowledge, to be aware of what one is, is already the beginning of wisdom, the beginning of understanding which releases you from time. . . . To be aware of, to get at that which IS, puts an end to struggle.*
>
> KRISHNAMURTI[1]

If we want to discover something more of the meaning of life—or if we want to survive as a species—we have to become more developed creatures than we are at present. We can only do this by getting a clearer knowledge of ourselves and of the directions in which we need to change those selves.

Mankind as a whole is more interested in the world around him and in how to change and conquer that, than in the world within. The origin of history of mental development, the significance and expansion of consciousness, these are matters generally regarded as too vague and intangible to be worthy of serious attention. We are now however in 'a situation very perilous' and this situation has its roots in human nature. It is to be profoundly hoped therefore that the magnitude of the crisis will awaken us to the fact that we can no longer afford to drift along in self-ignorance but must begin to take the human psyche as the most important of all objects of study. For if what happens in the external world is a result of what goes on in the mind of man, then we should start giving to mental processes the same scientifically careful observation as we have hitherto given to the exploration of the outer world. Only so can we redress the terrifying imbalance of a progress that has produced knowledge of nuclear fission but not the wisdom or power to control its use.

For some time now we have subscribed verbally to the fact,

[1] Khrishnamurti, *The First and Last Freedom*. London, Gollancz, 1961, p. 20.

taught by all great religions, that wisdom is to be sought within, but for the most part we have ignored the teaching, leaving our unregenerate egos to continue their scramble for possession and for power.

Shocked to the core by the cataclysm of the First World War, the church at that time was wont to insist, 'It is not Christianity which has failed; it is Christians'. True enough; but precisely how and where we had failed never became clear because then as now, introspection was regarded as morbid. It was easier to look for external causes in such things as over-population and economic misery where there was obviously plenty of scope for reform. Lest we repeat our mistake a third time, it would be as well to get clear at the start the difference between the sort of introspection which is morbid and the sort which is not.

People who are more interested in themselves than in the truth of things are morbid people whose development has been frustrated at some stage. But where concern with self is subordinate to concern for truth, the attempt to know and understand the self is wholesome, constructive, and necessary to further growth in understanding. Introspection in this scientific sense is a slow and difficult task but it slowly awakens us to some important discoveries which may be briefly stated as follows:

1. That we are not single and simple but are extremely complex entities, capable of ambivalent emotions.

2. That we are not static but are transitional creatures in process of becoming.

3. That we are not isolated beings complete in ourselves but that minds flow into and out from each other, influencing and being influenced by each other, and that in this sense we are in truth 'members one of another'.

4. That we are also parts of the Whole, the Cosmic Organism in which we live and move and have our being, from which our life flows and to which it is our destiny, when we have found our true selves, to become consciously related.

5. That the path to an increased knowledge of the nature of Ultimate Reality lies therefore not so much in the study of academic philosophy as in a deeper self-knowledge and self-development. In the process of achieving the latter, we shall be creating a fresh supply, however small, of the 'being' or leaven which may yet leaven the whole lump, and at the same time we shall be awakening to the perception that life is meaningful.

The impatient person who wants snap answers, the sceptic who questions the scientific validity of this approach, the defeatist who enjoys his pessimism, all these will at this point raise doubts and demand proofs for this claim. The sceptic may point to the fact that a great deal of evolution has been degenerative; that many animals, by developing exaggerated and restricting devices for their protection, have come to a dead end and that we, in our anxiety about security, appear to be going the same way; that even if we manage to survive, it is likely to be in a 1984 form of totalitarian society comparable at best to an ant heap.

It is quite true that there is no principle at work in life which will carry man *automatically* upward unless he himself makes the effort to acquire increase of consciousness. There is no trend that works inevitably in the right direction without his co-operation. But neither is there a trend working inevitably towards destruction. It is for man to choose where he will throw his weight, and in the fact that he can choose lies the first and greatest argument against despair.

The second is that, unlike the cockroach and all other armour-plated and over-specialised creatures, man has thus far managed to retain in some degree his suppleness and sensitivity and the ability to learn from his mistakes.

Thirdly he is the only animal to provide for his young a long and tenderly nurtured period of childhood and youth during which they may learn how to learn, how to become more conscious and adventurous individuals instead of other-directed mass-men. 'Children,' said Karl Gross, 'do not play because they are young, they are young in order that they may play', and through free play may develop their powers and capacities, especially that of learning how to live together. And lastly, man, through this freedom and opportunity for experiment, has developed a type of consciousness which is unknown in the animal world—the consciousness of himself, the ability not merely to observe the external world but to turn round on himself and ask 'Who am I?' 'What is life all about?' 'What is wrong with me or my species that we seek to destroy each other?'

But although man has achieved self-consciousness, he has as yet only a minimum of self-knowledge; and although he is able to ask questions about himself and his life, he is not able to answer them. Any who doubt this should listen carefully to the chance remarks that can be overheard in everyday conversation.

'What on earth made me say that? I could have bitten my tongue off as soon as I'd spoken.' 'Why did I do that? I love him like a brother: I swear it' (after calling his college friend a dirty nigger). And when asked why she was trying to escape from herself, a young woman replied, 'Myself; I've not the foggiest notion who or what that is. Maybe if I go a long way off into a different kind of environment, another world, I'll find out who I am, or whether I'm really anybody at all, or just a series of events in time . . . a psycho-physical process.'[1] 'Which of the six is the real man?' asked the confused officer Sergius of his conflicting selves. 'That is the question that torments me. One of them is a hero, another a buffoon, another a humbug, another perhaps a bit of a blackguard. And one, at least, is a coward; jealous, like all cowards.'[2]

There is no ready or easy answer to any of these questions for everyone must slowly and continuously seek out his own. That is the way to become an individual. The evolution of a new psychic centre which makes it possible to turn round on ourselves and ask such questions complicates life enormously but it is what makes further development possible. There are times when we would gladly evade the burden of a more complex selfhood. The price that must be paid for individuation seems altogether too heavy and we are tempted to indulge in 'uroboric incest'— i.e. the tendency to dissolve back to the condition when the ego was still contained in the unconscious and was as content as the embryo in the womb. We envy the animals who

> 'do not sweat and whine about their condition
> do not lie awake in the dark and weep for their sins.'[3]

for they are not torn with conflicting impulses and have not to endure uncertainty about the best course to pursue. They are single, whole, one-pointed and free from doubt and anxiety like Adam and Eve in the Garden.

But what sort of people were Adam and Eve? Before the alleged 'disobedience' they were not people at all, for personality only develops through effort and striving. The 'Fall' therefore was in fact a 'Rise', an advance into new knowledge and enlargement of

[1] Nancy Ross, *The Return of Lady Brace*. London, Collins, 1958, p. 219.
[2] G. B. Shaw, *Plays Pleasant and Unpleasant*, 'Arms and the Man'. London, Constable, 1898, p. 34.
[3] Walt Whitman.

consciousness. Of course, in later thought, somebody had to be blamed for bringing 'death into the world, and all our woe' and this ancient phantasy of the Fall has long served as a convenient whipping boy and formed the basis of the Christian mythos in the doctrine of original sin. But the goal for man is heightened consciousness, not the simple untested wholeness of the little child or of unconscious primeval man, but a mature wholeness at a higher level of being. Moreover however much we may hunger and yearn for the effortless ease of the Garden or for the peaceful life of the womb, we cannot in fact revert to that status. 'Uroboric incest' will not land us in Eden but in the degenerate condition described in some of Aldous Huxley's and Kafka's more terrible stories. It is not wise to try and put the clock back, to reverse the evolutionary process that has brought us thus far from the mud. We may permissibly look back in order to clarify the present or get new light on the future but to look back nostalgically because we are too lazy or too fearful to advance is to invite the fate of Lot's wife.

And because life is a continuous process, neither can we stand still. Bit by bit physics has had to give up a static conception of the world in favour of a dynamic one: 'Matter has been identified with energy and energy is sheer activity'.[1] What is true for physics must also be true for metaphysics. If matter is movement and activity, so is mind. Consciousness that becomes inert and static soon ceases to exist. We must always be in process of becoming whatever we have it in us to be. 'Becoming' is the operative word but hitherto in our impatience for end-products we have tried to side-step the becoming process. Our Victorian ancestors hoped that by dressing small children as 'little men and women' and imposing on them adult standards of behaviour, childishness could be short-circuited and the long becoming process, often irksome to the grown-up, be eliminated. This will not work: if the young are not permitted to become persons they will never be persons. The becoming process cannot be evaded. The same applies to the adult. The old are not automatically wise and there is no such thing as an educated person or, in any absolute sense, a mature person. The growth process is or should be continuous throughout life and it is foolish to think in terms of finishing schools. Education is never finished and the maturing

[1] A. N. Whitehead, *Nature and Life*. Cambridge University Press, 1934, p. 50.

process is never complete. The old have as much learning, growing and self-transforming to accomplish as the young, and the pitfalls into which self-ignorance can trap them may be even more serious and difficult to detect. We wrongly assume that since we are adult we know ourselves, or at least as much as we need to know. How far this is from the truth may be illustrated by the eminent theologian, Martin Buber. He tells of a dream which revealed to him how he was unconsciously deluding himself. In this dream he pictured himself standing before the Judgment Seat, awaiting the verdict on his life and work. Thunderous words came forth: 'Martin Buber, I ask you not: "Why were you not Moses?" "Why were you not Rabbi Baal Shem Tove?" I ask you only "Why were you not Martin Buber?"'

'Be yourself' is sound advice, but 'Know thyself' is equally necessary for without the information brought to him by the dream, Martin Buber would not have realized that he was trying to be someone else, that a hidden part of his mind was envious of others and trying to emulate them rather than to work towards his own true being.

It needs courage to accept these revelations and it needs insight to interpret the language of the educative dream. Indeed, until one has had the experience, it is difficult to believe that there is a part of one's mind more aware and more creatively active than the conscious self. This century has concentrated so exclusively on the facet of what is loosely called 'the unconscious' which is concerned with repressed complexes and instinctive forces, that other facets have been ignored. Yet it is true that,

> 'A self there is that listens in the heart
> To what is past the range of human speech,
> Which yet has urgent tidings to impart,
> The all but uttered and yet out of reach.'[1]

Not wholly out of reach to those who like Buber are sufficiently sensitive to respond to it.

Self-knowledge then involves knowledge of the non-conscious areas of the psyche as well as of the conscious, and such knowledge reveals the fact that we have within us the capacity for greater good as well as for greater evil than we know. 'We didn't know he had it in him' (spoken of unsuspected courage), illustrates the former, and the remark of the young soldier who slew

[1] Walter de la Mare.

his wife in his sleep: 'I had no desire to kill her' illustrates the latter. Well might R. L. Stevenson pray, 'We are evil, O Lord; help us to see it and amend. We are good; help us to be better.' But prayer alone will not do the trick; we have to work on ourselves. Vague General Confessions about having 'followed too much the devices and desires of our own hearts' mean precisely nothing unless we are clear as to the nature of those devices and desires. 'But I do not feel guilty' protest the young and the unaware. 'I don't make the wars; I have done no wrong. It is other people who cause the trouble.' Superficially speaking this may be true, but we are all members of the species, man, and therefore as Jung says, 'None of us stands outside humanity's black collective shadow'; none of us is wholly guiltless or without responsibility for the future if not for the past. The terrible fissures on the international scene cannot be healed until we cease tossing blame back and forth and try to deal with the split in our own nature. To remain in ignorance of destructive impulses, especially since psychology has given us the means for their realization, is as dangerous and as morally irresponsible as to leave powerful machinery unchecked, for it is human impulse that could stage world conflagration.

Can we awaken to this fact in time and what will awaken us? The prodigal son was reduced to eating with the swine before he 'came to himself'. Two world wars and nineteen years of 'running around on the brink of hell' since the last ended, leaves us in much the same rut, exercising much the same habits of thought and feeling that have twice plunged us into the abyss in this century. We recover and then proceed to drift along on the old track in contented self-ignorance towards a future we feel to be too far beyond our control for us to do anything about.

When that happy-go-lucky extrovert Peer Gynt was told by the Button-Moulder (Death) that he is now due to be melted down, that never having become a self, he is nothing save potential raw material, Peer laughs scornfully and replies: 'I've been myself all the days of my life . . . Peer all through.'

From the level of his immaturity and self-ignorance, this was true. He had lived out his impulses with zest and he had not deliberately harmed other people. Yet at the expense of others as well as of his own development, he had side-stepped all the learning, the pains, conflicts and tensions that are an inherent part of development. He was smugly satisfied with what he called his

'Gyntish self' as it was. When asked by Death, the Button Moulder, to say what he meant by that self he replied:

> 'It is the host
> Of wishes, appetites, desires—
> The Gyntish self. It is the sea
> Of fancies, exigencies, claims,
> All that in short makes my breast heave,
> And whereby I, as I, exist.'[1]

In other words Peer had identified with his instinctive urges. He was an inflated ego who had never seen the need for working on himself and therefore no growth had taken place in him. He was unaware of its own immaturity and without feeling of responsibility for his fellows or of debt to his society.

A seeker on the Quest once asked his guide: 'And if you don't succeed in paying your debt—what happens?' He was answered with a question: 'When a pullet doesn't begin laying at the proper age, what becomes of it?'[2] The same question was put by Death to Peer; and is now being put to mankind.

> 'Yourself you never have been at all
> Then what does it matter your dying out?'[3]

Clearly the area in which further evolution is most urgently needed is in the realm of self-understanding and self-transcending. In short, as Lewis Mumford has put it:

'The moment for another great transformation has come. If we shrink from that effort, we tacitly elect the post-historic substitute . . . To overcome the blind flight to automatism, mankind must deliberately resume the long effort that originally turned hominids into men.'[4]

[1] Henrik Ibsen, *Peer Gynt*, Act V.
[2] Daumal, *Mount Analogue*, V. Stuart, 1959.
[3] Ibsen, *op. cit.*
[4] Lewis Mumford, *The Transformations of Man.* London, Allen & Unwin, 1957, p. 138.

CHAPTER III

Self-Knowledge Through Self-Observation

It is the mind that can set man free . . .
This is not done by running away to
monasteries or mountains and spending
one's life there; it is done by USING THE
MIND TO ENQUIRE INTO ITS OWN OPERA-
TION.   PAUL BRUNTON[1]

If we agree that self-knowledge is the most important kind of knowledge to be acquired, we must next ask why its acquisition is so difficult of attainment. One answer is that the only self with which we are normally familiar, the conscious ego, is but a small part of the total psyche; that there are vast areas 'outside' consciousness, which are yet very actively influential on our conscious thoughts and feelings. The fact that with the greater part of these areas we can have no direct contact without the aid of the analyst makes the problem at first glance look hopeless. Yet since all great teachers such as the Buddha, Socrates and Jesus have stressed the basic importance of the Oracle's dictum, 'Know thyself', it would seem that even such limited knowledge of ourselves as we can acquire by ourselves must be worth the effort and that man can learn a great deal if he has the courage and humility to look honestly into himself. Moreover the willingness to do this and the realization of the necessity of self-observation and self-transformation are at least as important as the facts that may be unearthed. Incidentally the analyst's interpretation of those facts may vary and, still more serious, the will to good has been known to remain untouched at the end of long years of analysis in cases where the patient expected the work to be done for him rather than by him.

[1] Paul Brunton, *The Inner Reality*. London, Rider, 1957, p. 116.

So it is a momentous step forward in the evolution of the human psyche when a new centre or 'self' emerges which can, as it were, turn round on the old self and observe what goes on in the more marginal areas of consciousness, and can apply to them the same detached scrutiny as is employed by the physical scientist in his sphere.

The significance of this new psychological development is seen when placed in its evolutionary perspective. 'Man has slowly grown out of his animal origins. Slowly he climbs the ladder of evolution which at a certain point becomes a ladder of involution, a turning inward upon himself to discover consciously what he is and in the finding of that to become a new being, freed from the compulsions but not the empowering of ancient instinct.'[1]

This power to turn inward and observe himself is, psychologically speaking, a new 'mutation'. But we do not become new beings overnight as a result of it. Primitive passions remain but what we can say is that as a result of now being able, to some extent, to stand aside and observe them—even if only in retrospect—we are less identified with them and can get better command over them. Instead of saying ' "I" was angry', we can now say ' "I" was swept by a wave of anger'. Instead of ' "I" was afraid' we can say, ' "I" was overcome by fear'. The 'observing I' remains intact and as it grows stronger and more perspicacious, it will also grow more skilled at its task of acting as 'Charioteer', of controlling and directing the emotional life. The instinctive emotions are now seen not so much as my self but as my 'belongings' for which I must take responsibility. They are like raw material which has to be transmuted and its power made available for the new self that is trying to come to birth.

This integrative process cannot be swift or easy; in fact it is a kind of work which, once embarked on, will keep us busy for the rest of our lives. The goal is a much more difficult and complex kind of wholeness than that which we were obliged to leave behind in infancy when faced with the conflict between our own wishes and those of society. As a result of this early 'breach of the we', fears, anxieties and consequent hatreds inevitably begin to appear. There is no need to formulate a theological doctrine of 'original sin' to explain the existence of these anti-social emotions for they are the inescapable consequence of the growth process.

[1] Hugh l'Anson Faussett, *The Flame and the Light*. New York, Abelard-Schuman, 1963, p.23.

There is great need to get a better understanding of this process and a clearer knowledge of how the mind works in its totality, not merely at the surface levels. We are said to be the first generation to be conscious of the unconscious, but as yet this is a very dim consciousness indeed in most of us, and there is very little in our education which helps us to become more aware of what goes on in ourselves, of how to recognize the 'ravening wolf', to train it and redirect its energies instead of hiding it away as a monster whose existence cannot be admitted in civilized society.

The events of this century have revealed the abyss to which such blindness leads. We should know by now that, important as it is to work for political and social changes, it is not enough. Such external improvements will not of themselves cure our ills. So long as we continue to live in a cloud-cuckoo land of self-idealization, seeing the cause of tragedy only in other people or outer conditions; and so long as we fail to integrate the conscious ego with both the 'Shadow' self on the one hand and the potentially divine or true self in us on the other, the danger of fresh breakdown, individual or social or both, is always present. What is neglected in the psyche does not remain quietly passive, but eventually takes its revenge in the form of neurosis, psychosis, nihilism, crime, or the organized murder of war.

In August 1914, the dominant emotion in thoughtful people was one of incredulity. Having drifted along in the faith of the inevitability of progress, and in the happy assumption that among 'civilized' people wars were a thing of the past, they found it difficult to understand how this appalling thing could have happened. It took the penetrating insight of Freud to reveal the true situation. He wrote of that time, 'Our mortification and our grievous disillusionment regarding the uncivilized behaviour of our world compatriots in this war are shown to be unjustified. In reality our fellow-citizens have not sunk so low as we feared because they had never risen so high as we believed.'[1]

What was true of our world compatriots was true of all men including ourselves, but then as now it was easier and pleasanter to project the evil on to others and whitewash our own motives.

Long ago the Greeks with great discernment illustrated the tendency to self-idealization in the myth of Icarus—the youth who stuck wings on to his body in order to fly to the sun. The wings

[1] S. Freud, *Civilization, War and Death*. London, Hogarth Press, 1939, p. 11.

failed him because they were not a genuinely organic part of himself. Likewise high ideals which are mere verbal expressions rather than the product of personal effort and experience, will not stand the test of life. We do not get rid of hatred and aggression by covering them up; we merely become severed from our roots. The psyche can only make progress as an organic whole and ideals are worthless unless harmonized with instinctive levels of functioning. If the latter are left behind, forgotten and untransformed, sooner or later they will demand attention and expose us for the divided and hence the superficial and 'hollow' men that we are.

The Icarus in us must therefore be restrained from taking short cuts by way of dissociating from the more earthy aspects of ourselves for that is to court disaster. 'A borrowed plumage never grows,' and we are not entitled to function under a mask of virtue when, to quote Freud again, 'no ennoblement of instinct, no transformation of egoistic into altruistic inclinations has taken place'. When we do this, we live psychologically and spiritually beyond our means and shall fall to earth and have to start again, paying more attention next time to those primitive forms of behaviour which we ignored and repressed.

In passing, it should be noted that we tend to idealize not only ourselves but our friends, family, heroes, country and religion. We do this partly because they are 'ours', and whatever is ours can be used as material for ego-inflation; and partly because we are still at the level of what the late Dr Rivers termed 'All-or-one' thinking,[1] according to which there are only two categories—good and bad, black and white. X is a fine person or a rotter, a hero or a coward, a dominator or an appeaser and so on. Such over-simplification is not true to fact. More discriminating observation shows that personalities portray a blend of all human qualities in varying proportion and degrees; that a man may behave heroically in one situation and cravenly in another; that sometimes he seems imaginative and sometimes obtuse; kind and thoughtful to one, callous and cruel to another; dictatorial when he feels superior, cringing when he feels insecure. Even 'great' people are seldom great all the time or in all areas of their being. The name of Voltaire is known to all men because of his fierce hatred of injustice and his fearless fighting on behalf of those who suffered from it. Not so well known is the fact that he was also vain, unscrupu-

[1] W. H. R. Rivers, *Instinct and the Unconscious*. Cambridge University Press, 1920, p. 45, *passim.*

lous, jealous and lewd. A friend who knew him well described him as 'good to read and bad to know'.

Most of us do not like to analyse our friends in this way; it seems disloyal to them and diminishing to ourselves since they are 'ours'. Moreover too much frankness endangers friendship—as does too little. The widow's reply to the King was amusing, but in dubious taste.[1] Certainly the art of living together is the most difficult of all the arts, involving much tightrope balancing. Complete honesty is essential in all observations both of ourselves and others, but so is imagination, discrimination, restraint and sensitivity to the feelings of others. 'There is a time to keep silence and a time to speak',[2] and a failure in timeliness can be as fatal as a failure in honesty.

Increase of self-knowledge and self-integration will bring increase of discrimination, but at times, so deep has been the gulf between conscious ideals and unconscious lust for power that it has been possible for man to preach forgiveness and loving-kindness and at the same time to behave with abominable cruelty to those who differed from him. At the trial of St Joan, the English chaplain is so enraged at her unwillingness to accept the authority of his church that he is passionately eager to get her to the fire. After watching the burning he awakens to the horror of what he has done and as an old man excuses himself to his people with the words, 'You see, I did not know what cruelty was like'. He should have added, 'and I did not know I had these cruel impulses in me for I had never learnt to look at myself'.

St Paul did better in his frank recognition of the division which he found in his own nature: 'For though the will to do good is there, the deed is not. The good which I want to do I fail to do; but what I do is the wrong which is against my will' (Roman vii, 18).

'Oh make in me these civil wars to cease,' cried Sir Philip Sidney, but since we are not static animals like the termites[3] but creatures in process of change, the civil wars are inevitable for everyone who is involved in the growth process, who sees himself

[1] When handing the widow a posthumous medal in recognition of her husband's services to the State, a King commented on the privilege it must have been to live with such a great man. He received the startling reply: 'Your Majesty, he was insufferable'.

[2] Ecclesiastes iii, 7.

[3] Termites are said to have evolved their static and horribly 'successful' form of society 200,000,000 years ago.

as becoming, not as fixed and finished. Therefore Paul wisely did not let the conflict of forces within himself depress him unduly for he felt clear as to his purpose and direction: 'It is not to be thought that I have already achieved . . . but I press on, hoping to take hold of that for which Christ once took hold of me. I do not reckon myself to have got hold of it yet. All I can say is this: forgetting what is behind me, and reaching out for that which lies ahead, I press towards the goal.'

All this is but another way of expressing the Gospel teaching that we must lose ourselves to find them, a puzzling teaching if our concept of the self is of a single static entity rather than as a life which is growing from one level of being to another. The bewildered Peer Gynt, finally realizing there is no escape from the casting ladle, asks in his perplexity, 'What is it at bottom, this being onself?' The answer Death gave, 'To be oneself is to slay oneself', was as lost on Peer as it has been lost on most men who have not understood that the goal of life is the evolution of greater consciousness. The old King of the Trolls once asked Peer, 'What difference is there 'twixt trolls and men?', and answered his own question as follows:

> 'Out yonder under the shining vault
> Among men the saying goes: Man, be thyself.
>
> At home here with us amid the tribe of the trolls
> The saying goes: Troll, to thyself be—enough.'[1]

In other words, the non-human troll is content to stay as he is, but man must learn to transcend his present self and make the long journey through self-knowledge and self-transformation towards what the Prophet called the soul or the true self.

It is impossible to give in a diagram an accurate description of a living process. Yet just as a cross section of a tree, while telling us nothing of its life and beauty can yet give us some idea of its structure and functioning, so a cross-sectional diagram of the psyche can reveal a little of its complexity and of the fact that there are no absolute divisions, but that a kind of osmosis is always taking place between one level or area of the self and another. It also illustrates that by far the greater part of the self is still unconscious or non-conscious. Finally it indicates how easily the late offshoot of mind we call consciousness may be overwhelmed

[1] Ibsen, *Peer Gynt.*

by the immensity of the forces from which it has derived and how stupendous is its task of acting as guide and director to those forces and of bringing some degree of order and integration amongst them.

More than one diagram is given in order to stress the point that all are but tentative efforts to portray the complexity of what is yet a single inter-related whole.

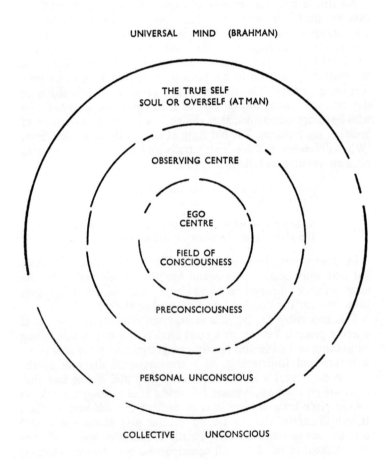

UNIVERSAL MIND (BRAHMAN)

THE TRUE SELF
SOUL OR OVERSELF (AT MAN)

OBSERVING CENTRE

EGO
CENTRE

FIELD OF
CONSCIOUSNESS

PRECONSCIOUSNESS

PERSONAL UNCONSCIOUS

COLLECTIVE   UNCONSCIOUS

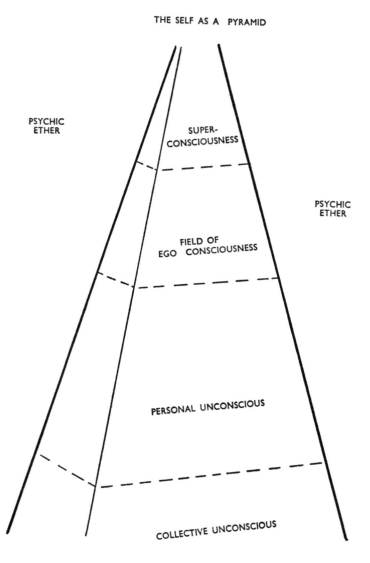

THE SELF AS A PYRAMID

PSYCHIC
ETHER

SUPER-
CONSCIOUSNESS

PSYCHIC
ETHER

FIELD OF
EGO CONSCIOUSNESS

PERSONAL UNCONSCIOUS

COLLECTIVE UNCONSCIOUS

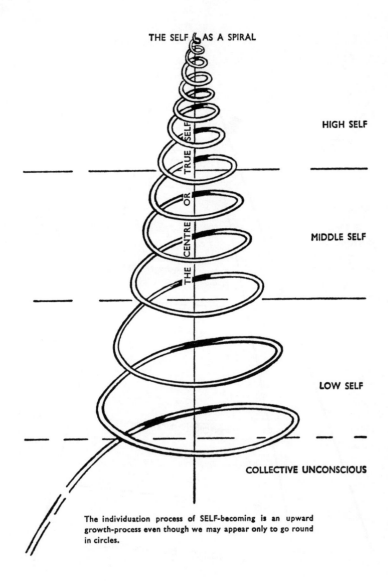

The individuation process of SELF-becoming is an upward
growth-process even though we may appear only to go round
in circles.

CHAPTER IV

The True Self

What does a man gain by winning the
whole world at the cost of his true self?

ST MARK viii, 36

It is easy enough to see that we have in us forces or drives
generally referred to as the instinctive self; also that we have a
more conscious organizing and observing ego-self. It is not so easy
to know what is meant by 'the true self', the finding of which is
said to be the most important thing in life. The authorized version
uses the word 'soul' rather than 'true self'. Is it possible to discover
within ourselves anything that could be called a soul? The
mechanist replies, 'No, the soul is not an empirical entity', and if
we look for the soul as a thing in itself—a psychological 'object'—
we shall not find it, for there is no such 'thing'. Unamuno says,
'We are not born into this world with souls, but the task for
which we are here is that each of us may win a soul'. We do not
however win a soul as a completed 'object', as the runner wins a
silver cup. The soul, spirit or true self is a matter of slow growth
and all we shall be able to find to begin with are rather faint
indications of its presence.

A thoughtful professor looking carefully into himself to discover whether mechanistic science had the last word, decided
that: 'Man is not all inheritance, man is also inspiration. What
makes me what I am is not simply the anthropoid ape who is my
honourable ancestor, not simply the instinct out of which my
life has come, *but the dim beginnings of new things in me*,[1] my
hopes, my aspirations, my heartfelt insights, the little emotions
stirring up the things I cannot name; that is me. Do not confine
me to the sexual impulse and the appetite for food. That is not all
there is of me.'[2]

[1] Tennyson expressed the same intuitive aspiration in *Maud*:
'And ah for a man to arise in me
That the man I am may cease to be.'

[2] Part of a lecture given in London University after World War I by the
late Professor Delisle Burns.

Most people would agree with the professor's self-analysis. Poetic licence may permit a Walt Whitman to say, 'I believe in you, my soul', but scientific introspection does not reveal the soul as a separate entity. It does however reveal those aspects or qualities of human nature which work upstream, the part of man that aspires, that responds to values and tries to realize them, the sense of responsibility, the capacity for self-sacrifice, the love of beauty and the passion for truth. The soul might therefore be defined as that aspect of man which is responsive to spiritual values.

Because the word 'spirit', like the word 'love', connotes a variety of meanings, and because of its close association with matters theological, the psychologist not unnaturally tends to fight shy of its use lest he be regarded as 'unscientific'. Yet in spite of all its ambiguities, 'spirit' is a time-honoured word, and in any case we have no other with which to denote those forces in man which conflict with his instinctive forces and which are concerned with higher values than those of the senses.

Jung has clearly stated the difference as follows: 'I do not doubt that the natural instincts or drives are forces of propulsion in human life, whether we call them sexuality or the will to power; but I also do not doubt that these instincts come into collision with the spirit, for they are continually colliding with something, and why should not this something be called spirit? I am far from knowing what spirit is in itself, and equally far from knowing what instincts are. The one is as mysterious to me as the other, yet I am unable to dismiss the one by explaining it in terms of the other.'[1]

And yet, although instinct and spirit do in fact continuously 'collide' with each other, so that 'The things I would not, them I do', the difference between them is not absolute. The one has developed from the other and each is necessary to the other. Instinct is of course basic to life, yet it is through transcending instinct and using its power in new directions that the soul or true self develops. There are no hard and fast lines to be drawn in the evolutionary process but there is throughout creation, a continuous striving[2] towards fuller life. The Yale biologist,

[1] Jung, *Modern Man in Search of a Soul*, p. 137.
[2] Perhaps this was in the mind of the writer of the Epistle to the Romans (viii, 22) when he said, 'We know that the whole created universe groans in all its parts as if in the pangs of childbirth'.

Edmund Sinnott, points out that there is already in the plant that from which human consciousness develops, and that 'Man's spirit is the highest expression of what began as the formative self-regulating quality in all living stuff'.[1]

This evolutionary viewpoint which sees the spirit of man as having its origin in the striving and aspiring character of life itself, rather than as something totally new and peculiar to man, breaks down our static concepts and reveals our destiny as growth towards new life. It also reveals that we are parts of the Great Process and that, having achieved consciousness, we may, if we choose, co-operate with that Process by trying to actualize the spiritual possibilities latent within us.

Such increase and strengthening of the life of the spirit has always been, officially at least, one of the concerns of the higher religions, though not always alas their primary concern as it was with the great Masters. These all had the same goal—the awakening of man to an awareness of the potential new life or 'true self' within him. It was for this reason that Socrates called himself a midwife. The so-called gnostic religions had the same purpose and tried to teach men, through such rituals as the Eleusinian Mysteries, the significance of rebirth and of dying to live. It is not an easy lesson. Even that Master in Israel[2] could not grasp it, and the verdict of the Greek Teachers was that, 'Many bear the palm, but few are the mystes': many attend the ritual but few understood its meaning. The same is true of all who observe external ceremony but give only lip service to the Teaching. Hence the sad history of the Christian Church and the sad condition of twentieth-century man.

The power of words for good or ill is enormous. When we use words with insufficient thought, there is grave danger that we may blind ourselves into thinking we are that to which we verbally subscribe. Everyone would consent to St. Paul's statement that, 'The Harvest of the Spirit is love, joy, peace, patience, kindness, goodness, fidelity and self-control'.[3] But we cannot have these things just by subscribing to them or praying for them. We cannot have fruits without roots or a harvest without growth,

[1] Edmund W. Sinnott, The Biology of the Spirit. New York, Viking Press, 1955, p. 136.
[2] Nicodemus was puzzled and asked, 'How can these things be?' See John iii, 10.
[3] Galatians v, 22. N.E.B.

and it is the difficulty of growing these desirable qualities that receives insufficient attention. Some of the blackest pages in history have been written by men who failed to see the distinction between religious language and religious living. Men like Torquemada and Caiaphas are but two examples amongst the many who have used religious language as a cover for their disreputable emotions. Still more of us fail to see the dissociation that can so easily take place between our words and our lives. It was said of one preacher, 'He talked so much of heaven that he was of no earthly use'. Lofty words must be related to earthly conditions or, like the Greek Anteus, they lose their power.[1]

Man is in fact confronted with the strange and incredibly difficult task of learning to live simultaneously in two worlds. He is

'A swinging wicket, set between
The unseen and the seen.'

This means he has not merely to go back and forth from the one to the other; he has to relate them as did Brother Lawrence, and St. John of the Cross of whom it was said that 'he was fully capable of doing business with this world while being all the time a man of the next'. In other words we have to learn how to set our affection and our attention on 'things above' even as we deal with things of the earth. The spirit must find its dwelling place in our mundane thoughts and deeds, or it will avail us nothing to externalize, personify and worship it as the Paraclete or the Third Person of the Trinity. Spirit, however we envisage it, must be tested out in living. If it is just a name for a remote and unrelated 'Something' existing somewhere in space, it is of no use to us. But if it is experienced as another dimension of being into which we can enter, this gives support and significance to our everyday lives.

As he hung on the cross, Christ saw that his tormentors were to be forgiven because they were dissociated within themselves. 'They know not what they do',[2] was the utterance of profound

[1] Anteus was invincible so long as he kept his feet in contact with the earth. In one battle with Hercules, however, he allowed himself to be lifted in the air, whereupon all his strength left him and he was quickly defeated.

[2] The indictment of the Pharisees was: 'You clean the outside of the cup and plate; but inside there is nothing but greed and wickedness . . . you pay tithes of mint and rue . . . but have no care for justice and the love of God'. St Luke xi, 39-40. N.E.B.

psychological insight but we have not yet taken it seriously and applied it to the dissociation between word, thought and deed that exists in ourselves. Eastern religions have developed techniques for increasing self-knowledge and bringing dubious motives under observation. We of the West tend to be supercilious about Yoga methods of self-training and it may be that they are not altogether suited to our more extroverted temperament. But our Westernized form of Christianity was Eastern in origin, and, according to the Gospels, Christ also stressed the discipline of the inner life rather than the observance of outer ritual and affirmed that, 'As a man thinketh in his heart, so is he'.

'As a man thinketh.' The trouble is that we do very little thinking for ourselves or about ourselves and such as we do is mainly superficial. The result is that we drift into ever more appalling disasters. Sometimes these shake us out of our complacency and in some natures achieve undreamed of heights of courage and self-transcendence under their suffering. Dr Viktor Frankl tells of his discovery of the spirit of man coming to birth amid the horrors of the concentration camps, a discovery which led him to the conviction that psychotherapy must be spiritually-centred if it is to deal effectively with the whole man.

In those camps conditions were so appalling that life seemed reduced to a desperate struggle for existence. Everything in them conspired to degrade man and rob him of his will and human dignity. Yet in the midst of this horror of sadism and cruel distress, Frankl found that there were men of such heroic stature that they could not be shaken by the kicks, cruelty, weariness and starvation, but were able in some degree to transcend their surroundings and preserve spiritual freedom. He writes:

'We who lived in concentration camps can remember the men who walked through the huts comforting others, giving away their last piece of bread. They may have been few in number, but they offer sufficient proof that everything can be taken away from a man but one thing; the last of the human freedoms—the freedom to choose one's attitude in any given set of circumstances, to choose one's way.'[1]

He tells of a young boy who instead of protesting at life's treatment of him, perceived that life was offering him a chance to face death in a courageous and dignified way; and of a dying woman

[1] Frankl: *op. cit.*, p. 65.

who said to him, 'I am grateful that fate has hit me so hard. In my former life I was spoiled and did not take spiritual accomplishments seriously.'

Both these victims felt that they were being challenged by life, and they were able to meet the challenge by entering the dimension of spirit.

When therefore we feel overwhelmed by the cruelty in the world and are tempted to despair of human nature, we should remember not only the evil genius that can invent such things as gas chambers but the spirit of man that can rise triumphant over pain and evil and enable men to walk upright to their dreadful death with songs of prayer and praise upon their lips; we should remember not only the lust for power that will tolerate no questioning but the quiet unflinching courage of such scientists as Giordano Bruno who, under the rule of the 'Holy Office' of the Inquisition endured seven years in a dungeon rather than deny what he knew to be true, and who when finally taken out to be burned alive, could say to his inhuman judges: 'I prefer a spirited death to a cowardly life'. Earlier he had written, 'There are men in whom the working of the will of God is so powerful that neither threats nor contumely can cause them to waver'.

It is not surprising that Frankl, as a result of the courageous spirit he observed in Hitler's prison camps, should reach the conclusion that 'man is more than psyche' and that psycho-analysis is incomplete without psycho-synthesis, that is, without awakening in man his true self or spiritual self—his courage to suffer and his will to find meaning in that suffering as in all life. Only by such awakening can man lose that sense of life's meaninglessness which, says Frankl, 'is the mass neurosis of our day'.

There remains one last question of profoundest importance. In the process of finding his true self, does man find anything more? Is the spirit of man related to a Spirit of the Universe? This is what religions teach, but to know it, as distinct from believing it, the individual needs to feel it as true in his own experience. The humanist, like the Stoic, believes in the spirit of man; he does not believe in the supernatural; he does not believe there is 'Someone' or 'Something' behind and beyond the state of being known to us through our senses in the here and now. Man therefore, he maintains, must 'go it alone'. The search for meaning by reference to other possible realms of being is nothing but a consolatory phantasy.

The desire not to delude oneself with phantasies is to be respected, but it is possible to fall over backwards in this anxiety to preserve one's intellectual integrity; it is possible to be negatively as well as positively dogmatic. There is no proof that the universe is a meaningless process, and minds as careful to avoid self-deception as that of William James say that as man journeys in the spirit, he finds that 'spirit with Spirit can meet', that 'he becomes conscious that this higher part of himself is co-terminous and continuous with a More of the same quality which is operative in the universe outside of him and which he can keep in working touch with and in a fashion get on board of'.[1]

In the following chapter we shall make the acquaintance of some of those who have actually made the breakthrough into this 'More'.

[1] William James, *Varieties of Religious Experience*, being the Gifford Lectures on Natural Religion, delivered at Edinburgh 1901-1902. London, Longmans, Green, p. 499.

CHAPTER V

Cosmic Consciousness

O World Invisible, we view thee,
O World Intangible, we touch thee.[1]
                    FRANCIS THOMPSON

The fact that in the course of evolution man has developed not
only the power of reasoning but the capacity for spiritual apprehension and aspiration, should give us good grounds for faith in
the possibilities of the future. Yet at the present time there is
much pessimism about the future. Having lost faith in the old
assurances that 'God's in His Heaven' and having observed the
depressing spectacle of humanity 'running around on the brink of
hell' in the grooves of habitual patterns of thought and behaviour,
we tend to share the defeatism of the preacher: 'That which is
done is that which shall be done'.[2] We feel trapped by our own
natures into following a circular course from which neither the
Christianity of the churches nor any other 'ism' can save us.

Yet we have already been given the answer as to how a breakthrough can be made and faith in life be renewed.

From time to time there have appeared on the earth men and
women who have achieved a state of consciousness and a spiritual
stature far surpassing that of the majority of ordinary individuals,
but a state to which all may aspire.

Some two thousand years ago a spiritual Pioneer generally
regarded by His followers as divine, or if not divine, at least 'the
greatest of the sons of men',[3] taught that the purpose of life was
the seeking and finding of this state of being which he called
symbolically the Kingdom of God or the Kingdom of Heaven. He
said that this Kingdom was within us and around us, that the

[1] 'The Kingdom of God' from *Selected Poems of Francis Thompson*.
London, Burns & Oates, 1908.
[2] Ecclesiastes i, 10.
[3] H. D. Oliver, 'Greatest of the Sons of Men'. A pamphlet published by
the Union of Modern Free Churchmen, Crawley Down, Sussex.

way to it was strait and narrow and found only by the few, but that it was in fact the 'pearl of great price' for the possession of which a merchant might well sacrifice everything that he owned. Others before Jesus had referred to this condition as illumination, brahmic bliss, samdahi, nirvana, satori, etc. In the West, it is generally spoken of as mystic experience, ecstasy or cosmic consciousness.

To be told 'Few there be that find it' would be depressing were it not for the fact that the mode of evolution appears as 'The higher the fewer'. But all, however lowly their achievement, can have their feet on the road that leads to fuller life. To be a seeker is what matters. One will not find all the answers but one will find something—enough Light for the next step. There is the encouraging promise that 'He who seeks finds, and to him who knocks the door will be opened',[1] even if only by a crack.

Unfortunately the attention and interest of most men, especially those of the West, is more concerned with the outer things of time and space than with inner development. They have therefore found it simpler and easier to envisage the young Prophet as a Man-God to be worshipped than to explore the inner meaning of His teaching about the nature of the Kingdom and the way thereto through the difficult process of the expansion and deepening of consciousness. After a hundred years of dispute, biological evolution is now generally accepted as a fact, but the evolution of *mind* towards fuller enlightenment is little considered—and this in spite of the realization that it is our spiritual immaturity that makes possible the slaughtering of man by man. Orthodox religion is still more interested in the propagation of beliefs than in the education of the emotions. In this respect the work of the psychological clinic is often more genuinely religious than the work of the church. Eventually the two will work in harmony.

The sceptic who has never experienced anything akin to ecstasy, and the pure rationalist who claims that reason is the only approach to knowledge, will be very dubious about the reports of the mystic and will tend to dub him an escapist indulging in phantasy in order to cut himself off from the trials and miseries of life. The exact opposite is the truth. Christ's teaching that the Way is no primrose path has been confirmed by all true mystics, ancient and modern. Among the latter we have the words of the poet Alice Meynell, 'Endless the Way, followed

[1] St Matthew vii, 8.

with how much pain', and Plotinus of the third century wrote in a letter to his friend:

'The Egyptian priests used to tell us that a single touch with the wing of their holy bird could charm the crocodile into torpor; it is not thus speedily that the pinions of your soul will have power to still the untamed body. The creature will yield only to watchful, strenuous constancy of habit. Purify your soul from all undue hope and fear about earthly things, deny self-affections and appetites, and the inner eye will begin to exercise its clear and solemn vision.'[1]

This must not be taken to mean that the Way is one of bleak ascetism and renunciation. At the start of his inward journey the Buddha tried this and found that it did not work. Entering into the 'life more abundant' is not attained by continuous self denial; it is also a joyous adventure irradiated by glimpses of 'Heaven'. The disciplines involved are more akin to those willingly undertaken by the athlete in order to become skilled in his own sphere.

To the rationalist who asks for proof, Plotinus replies that the Infinite cannot be known by reason.

'It is the office of reason to distinguish and define. The Infinite therefore cannot be ranked among its objects. You can only apprehend the Infinite by a faculty superior to reason, by entering into a state in which you are your finite self no longer—in which the divine essence is communicated to you. This is ecstasy. It is the liberation of your mind from its finite consciousness.'[2]

It is encouraging to find a well-known rationalist himself warning against too narrow or negative an attitude on this matter. Speaking of the mystic experience, he says: 'I have no wish to deny it, nor even to declare that the insight which reveals it is not a genuine insight. What I wish to maintain . . . is that insight, untested and unsupported, is an insufficient guarantee of truth, in spite of the fact that much of the most important truth is first suggested by its means . . . Reason is a harmonizing, controlling force, rather than a creative one. Even in the most purely logical realm it is insight that first arrives at what is new.'[3]

[1] Letter of Plotinus to Flaccus, 188: 78-81, quoted from Richard Bucke, *Cosmic Consciousness*, New York, Dutton, 1901, pp. 121-3.
[2] *Ibid.*
[3] Bertrand Russell, *Mysticism and Logic*, London, Allen & Unwin, 1917.

The major test of the validity of mystic insight is the quality of life of those claiming to have had experience of it. Mystics who have made the deepest impact were not only good, wise, imaginative and brave; many have had intellectual capacity above the average. As an example we may take Professor A. N. Whitehead, collaborator with Russell in the writing of *Principia Mathematica*: He says:

'Most of what we think and say with our conscious minds and speech is shallow and superficial. Only at rare moments does that deeper and vaster world come through into conscious thought or expression. They are the memorable moments of our lives, when we feel—when we know—we are being used as instruments of a greater force than ourselves for purposes higher and wider than our own.'[1]

That is the mystic's fundamental insight — that the visible world is but one part or aspect of an invisible, super-sensible, 'spiritual' universe from which it draws its sustenance and its significance, and that union with this higher and mainly unknown Reality is our true end. The poet's paradox, 'O world invisible, we view thee', strikes a responsive chord in the hearts of all who have known, however dimly, this greater Reality, as do his other words:

'I dimly guess what Time in mists confounds;
Yet ever and anon a trumpet sounds
From the hid battlements of Eternity;
Those shaken mists awhile unsettle, then
Round the half-glimpsed turrets slowly wash again.'[2]

How dimly or how vividly we glimpse this vaster world will depend on how far the level of consciousness has been raised in ourselves. In a few men the true Self or spirit has evidently become sufficiently developed to make contact with the Spirit of the Universe so that they have experienced a union expressed in such words as: 'I and the Father are one', 'Become what thou art; thou art That', 'Find thou but thy Self, thou art I', or, as the 'pagan' Plotinus put it, 'Then the soul neither sees, nor distinguishes by seeing, nor imagines that there are two things; but becomes as it were another thing, ceases to be itself and belong to

[1] Lucien Price, *Dialogues of A. N. Whitehead*, Boston, Little, Brown, 1954, p. 369.
[2] Francis Thompson, 'The Hound of Heaven'.

itself. It belongs to God and is one with Him, like two concentric circles: concurring they are one; but when they separate, they are two . . . (Since) in this conjunction with Deity, there were not two things, but the perceiver was one with the thing perceived.'[1]

This perfect and ecstatic union is the end of the journey. It can only be described in figurative language since, as Goethe said, 'The highest cannot be spoken'. One of the greatest stumbling blocks to understanding the religion of the mystic, which is the religion of the Gospels, lies in our difficulty in distinguishing between the literal and the symbolic. Once this difference were grasped, all futile argument about the existence of God, the divinity of Jesus, or the immortality of the soul would come to an end. It has been truly said that no literalist can enter the Kingdom of Heaven, the reason being that ability to see behind the literal to its hidden meaning is a condition of entry.

The parables of Jesus are all expressed in symbolic terms which are meaningless unless we awaken to the inner significance. 'The Kingdom' for example is 'not of this world', neither is it an astronomical location; it is 'the leaven that leaveneth the whole lump' the 'treasure hid in a field'; in other words it is a state of consciousness which, when achieved, gives meaning to life in an experience of 'Heaven'. Everything is seen differently and the conviction is unassailable that, as Juliana of Norwich expressed it, 'All manner of things shall be well' or in the words of a living mystic, 'Of course since that is true, nothing else matters'.

This does not mean that henceforth the journey of life is a thing of uninterrupted glory and wonder. What has been 'seen' is but partial and fleeting, and back in the world of ten thousand things to which it is essential that we return, for there is no spiritual health in flight from life, the memory of the vision may fade and the temptation come to question its validity. The realization of this danger caused the Psalmist to cry 'If I forget thee O Jerusalem, let my right hand forget her cunning'. For the mystic knows that to doubt or forget the gift of this experience would be the ultimate disloyalty, 'the sin against the Holy Ghost' or Spirit of life.

We may say then that in so far as the individual is on the way towards finding his 'soul' or true self, he is also on the way

[1] Quoted by Marghanita Laski in *Ecstasy*, London, Cressett Press, 1961. p. 124.

towards finding something more, namely a relationship of his Self
to Something or Someone beyond himself; to That in Which, or
in Whom 'we live and move and have our being' the true life of
all. Such a realization makes it permissible to return to a symbolic
use of the personal pronoun as does Emily Brontë in her brave
Last Lines which dismiss the fear of death and destruction as
irrelevant in the light of That which transcends both.

> 'There is no room for death
> Nor atom that His might could render void,
> Thou, Thou art being and breath,
> And what Thou art can never be destroyed.'

'I was waiting for you,' cried the dying Plotinus to his friend,
before that which is divine in me departs to unite itself with the
divine in the universe.'[1]

The Rabbi is reported as saying that those who find the pathway into new life with this degree of certainty are few.[2] This is
because only a few achieve the level of consciousness which makes
it possible. 'Like can only apprehend like' and we are not as yet
very much like the values to which we subscribe. A babe in the
cradle cannot appreciate the music of Bach and a worm in the
soil cannot know the life of the bird. In our spiritual development,
despite all our knowledge and skill, we are at the level of the babe
and the worm. Therefore instead of the ecstasy of perfect knowledge, we can only see 'as through a glass darkly'.[3] It may be
asked, 'If the experience comes suddenly to some, why should it
not come to all?' The answer is that it only comes where there
has been long study, deep thinking, loving service. A continuous
preparation and self-discipline preceded Dr Richard Bucke's vision[4]

[1] Quoted by Dr Kenneth Walker in *The Conscious Mind*, London, River,
1962, p. 91.
[2] St Matthew vii, 13.
[3] I Corinthians xiii. N.E.B.
[4] Richard Bucke, *op. cit.*, p. 10. 'Directly afterwards came upon him a
sense of exultation, of immense joyousness accompanied by an intellectual
illumination quite impossible to describe . . . Among other things . . .
he saw and knew that the Cosmos is not dead matter but a living Presence,
that the soul of man is immortal, that the universe is so built and ordered
that without any peradventure all things work together for the good of
each and all . . . He claims that he learned more within the few seconds
during which the illuminations lasted than in previous months or even
years of study, and that he learned much that no study could ever have
taught. Into his brain had streamed one momentary lightning flash of the
brahmic splendour which has ever since lightened his life.'

as it must have preceded the incident on the Mount of Transfiguration. The 'pinions of the soul' can only grow on those
equipped to wear them. 'Unless there is a suitable endowment
within, the Tao will not abide, the Voice will not be heard.'[1]

If therefore we want to become 'seers' there is nothing for it
but to work at cleansing the mirror of what Blake called 'the
Doors of Perception', in other words at achieving sufficient inner
development and clarity for the Light to shine through us. We
reverse the existent order when we pray 'Send out Thy light and
Thy truth'; for they are already here, around us and within,
enfolding us like an atmosphere. The Old Testament poet was
right to ask 'Whither shall I go from Thy spirit, or whither shall
I flee from Thy presence?' If everything in life is organically
related to the Life Spirit pervading all, then it must be our un-
readiness that keeps us ignorant of the fact that our task in this
life-span must be to become more perceptive and aware. Meister
Eckhart assured his people that 'God is bound to act as soon as
He shall find thee ready'; and Shakespeare observed 'The readiness
is all'.

Meanwhile we can be grateful for such glimpses of 'the many-
splendoured Thing' as do manage to penetrate 'our clay-shuttered
doors', whether these are nothing more than the rose in bloom
or the song of the lark, they are the 'dim beginnings' of that
higher consciousness which will eventually tell us all we need to
know.

Unlike the teachers thus far mentioned, there are some who
believe that man's evolution will *automatically* bring him to this
experience of Cosmic Consciousness, and indeed that 'this step in
evolution is even now being made'.[2] This can hardly be so for the
simple reason that the advent of self-consciousness has brought
with it the power of choice and a power that is not used will
atrophy. Therefore unless we *choose*

> 'Cherishingly to tend and feed and fan
> That inward fire, whose small precarious flame,
> Kindled or quenched, creates
> The noble or the ignoble men we are',[3]

we can only sink back to the mud and allow evolution to

[1] Lao-tzu

[2] Richard Bucke, *op. cit.*, p. 3.

[3] Aldous Huxley, *Orion: The Cicadas and Other Poems*, New York,
Harper & Bros.

degenerate into devolution. Even a mystic of the spiritual stature of Tagore often found himself distressed at the ease with which the spark or cosmic sense can be smothered by the trivialities of daily life; at how the weight of material concerns can drag our minds away from attending to the significant. He says: 'This gravitational pull hurts me almost every day . . . I feel it very much: I struggle against it . . . How painfully homesick I am, not for any geographical spot, but for a place where it would be quite simple for me to stand face to face with the Infinite.' He once wrote of his own mystic experience, 'For a moment I saw as it were into the heart of the Infinite where every thing and person fell together into a new and significant kind of relationship'.

On one of the many occasions when Jesus was trying to explain to his hearers the meaning of the Way and the Goal, he told them 'Unless you turn round and become like children, you will never enter the Kingdom of Heaven'.[1] Little children have a wholeness and singleness of heart which is inevitably lost in the perplexities inherent in the growth process, but which may eventually be recovered in a new form if we win through to an integration at a higher level. The way to this new wholeness is the way of humility. 'Let a man humble himself till he is like this child.'[2] That is to say, let him see himself as he is, admitting his immense ignorance, and his many defects, and at the same time let him be open to the mystery of life and explore it with the interest and wonder of the child.

Growth towards maturity necessitates the breaking of the 'Adamic' ecstasy, the untroubled bliss of early life. Sooner or later all men must be driven from the sheltered Garden to face long and arduous journeyings. It is futile to look back nostalgically to a stage that is past for that is to resist the law of growth. But if we go forward we shall ultimately find that:

> 'the end of all our exploring
> Will be to arrive where we started,
> And know the place for the first time.'[3]

But to know it with a difference; for to have made such a journey is to have completed, not a circle, but a stage in a spiral. It is to have integrated in some degree the emotional underworld with

[1] Matthew xxiii, 4.
[2] Matthew xxiii, 12.
[3] T. S. Eliot, 'Little Gidding'.

CHAPTER VI

Symbolism in Religious Thinking

> Every truth apprehended by finite intelligence must by its very nature only be the husk for a deeper truth.
>
> C. SPURGEON: *Mysticism in English Literature*[1]

> I do not think the Christian myth has anything left to tell Western man unless he understands it outside in . . . the pilgrimage is not a journey into the future but into the Centre.
>
> ALAN WATTS: *Myth and Ritual in Christianity*[2]

In his attempt to help man towards a deeper understanding of life, Jesus gave much of his teaching in the form of parable and allegory. In so doing he revealed the analogy between the natural and the spiritual, between the laws governing the external world and the laws of the inner life. 'Except a grain of wheat fall into the earth and die, it abideth by itself alone; but if it die, it beareth much fruit.'[3] New and fuller life is only available to those prepared to 'die' to customary habits of thought, to risk the security of the known path.

God, the source and meaning of life, says Jesus, surrounds you everywhere. You can discover the significance of spiritual law

[1] Cambridge University Press, 1927.
[2] London and New York, Thames & Hudson, 1953, p. 81 *passim*.
[3] St John xii, 24.

from what you observe in the natural. All truth is there awaiting your perception of it. The seeing eye will find with Blake

'a world in a grain of sand
And Heaven in a wild flower'

and the reflective mind will discover in all things visible

'correspondence to that spirit world
Outside the limits of our space and time,
Whereto we are bound'.

The correspondence holds of course in the 'bad spiritual' as well as the good. The insect that feeds on the larva of other insects exhibits one blatant kind of parasitism; the 'devouring mother' who satisfies her own emotional needs from the lives of her children, displays another, a more subtle and harmful kind.

When therefore a person says of religion: 'It doesn't mean a thing to me', it does not follow that no meaning is there. The defect is in the person, in the misunderstanding of what religion is, and in the failure of his teachers to give enlightenment. Few people can make their spiritual discoveries unaided. When Philip asked the Ethiopian eunuch on the road to Gaza: 'Understandest thou what thou readest?' (the book in question being that of Isaiah the prophet), the eunuch not surprisingly replied: 'How can I except some man should guide me?' Many a perplexed listener to the church 'Lessons' would like to ask the same question: 'How do you expect me to make sense of this unless you explain what it means?'

Thoughtful man does desperately want to make sense of life, to find it meaningful, especially in its painful aspects. Indeed he must find meaning there if at all since to live is to suffer. No adequate why has yet been given to the problem of suffering, but we shall get a little nearer to one if we think of religion as the search for meaning rather than as the expression of historic fact or theological doctrine. There is no need to discard all doctrine provided we understand its inner significance where this exists, but if we fail to do so, it is valueless. The doctrine of the Assumption of the Blessed Virgin Mary appears as idolatry to the literal-minded Protestant. Viewed allegorically, however, it can suggest the elevation of the feminine principle to equality of status with the male.[1]

[1] see C. G. Jung, *Answer to Job*, Chapter XIX. Routledge and Kegan Paul.

Both agnostic and believer need to understand the Christian mythos 'outside-in' and so replace disputation by a deepening of insight into truths which have universal validity. Myth and symbol should be regarded as the poetry of religion, but when taken as literal truth their deeper significance is lost. It is very unfortunate that the word 'myth' should be defined in the Oxford Dictionary as 'purely fictitious narrative' for this ignores the meaning hidden in the narrative. To miss this meaning is to miss the point, the essential kernel of the story, parable or mythos. 'Christianity' as taught by Jesus is not debatable; his parables expressed the deep truths about life, death, birth, suffering and growth. It was these meaningful truths that he was primarily concerned to convey. But truths of meaning are harder to perceive than truths of external fact and the Master appears to have been perplexed by the obtuseness of his own disciples. When Peter asked: 'Declare unto us the parable', he replied: 'Are ye also even yet without understanding? Perceive ye not . . . ' That was the trouble—an inadequate depth of understanding. It is still the trouble.

After nearly two thousand years we still do not know the things that belong to our peace. It is so much easier to centre one's religious feelings in the adolescent adoration of a Person and on the belief in the literal truth of the mythos that has been built up around that Person than to awaken to and wrestle with the hidden meaning of his teaching.

'The first step towards the non-religion of the Western world was made by religion itself. When it defended its great symbols, not as symbols but as literal stories, it had already lost the battle. In doing so the theologian . . . helped to transfer the powerful expressions of the dimension of depth into objects or happenings on the horizontal plane. There the symbols lose their power and meaning and become an easy prey to physical, biological and historical attack.'[1] This has been all too terribly demonstrated, not only in the bloodstained history of the literalist religions that have cared more for the triumph of their doctrines and the extension of their church than for the increase of inner growth in understanding, but in the fact that Christian and ex-Christian countries live in a perpetual state of internecine warfare, active or 'cold'.

The first step then towards an increase in religious vitality is

[1] Paul Tillich, 'The Lost Dimension in Religion', *Saturday Evening Post*, June 14, 1958.

the realization that our symbols have gone dead on us because we have lazily treated them as expressions of outer fact rather than of inner meaning. 'The standpoint of the Creeds,' says Jung, 'is archaic: they are full of impressive mythological symbolism which, if taken literally, comes into insufferable conflict with knowledge. But if, for instance, the statement that Christ rose from the dead is to be understood not literally but symbolically, then it is capable of interpretations that do not collide with knowledge and do not impair the meaning of the statement. The objection that understanding it symbolically puts an end to the Christian's hope of immortality is invalid, because long before the coming of Christianity mankind believed in a life after death and therefore had no need of the Easter event as a guarantee of immortality. The danger that a mythology understood too literally, and as taught by the Church, will suddenly be repudiated lock, stock and barrel is today greater than ever. Is it not time that the Christian mythology, instead of being wiped out, was understood symbolically for once?'[1]

At the same time, Jung warns the rationalists that they should be careful what they throw away, for while the *literal* interpretation of the creeds is archaic, nevertheless as *symbols* they 'possess a life of their own on account of their archetypal character'. Therefore our interest should lie not in proving or disproving their literal truth but in exploring their hidden meaning. Only so can the gulf between faith and reason be bridged. It has been suggested that what our day needs is a new set of symbols to interpret reality to us and make it meaningful. True there must be endless new symbols of truth awaiting our discovery of them, but they will not be arrived at by a process of conscious reasoning. Far more important than finding new symbols is learning to understand the meaning of the symbols we already have, and learning to think in terms of symbol, myth, allegory, parable; to seek out the deep significance of the words we use in our liturgies so that they do not become mere words, empty of meaning and subject to 'vain repetition'.

The Christian story, when insisted on as literal truth necessary to salvation, becomes subject matter for endless debate if nothing worse; but as a mythos hiding deep truths it is a thing of fascination and inspiration, an earthly vessel containing the heavenly treasure.

[1] C. G. Jung, *The Undiscovered Self*, Boston, Little Brown, 1957-8, pp. 37-8.

Let us explore briefly some of the hidden truths of value and of meaning in the mythos itself.

The Fall of Man

Since man became capable of thought, he has been faced by the mystery of suffering and has evolved myths to explain it. The simplest of these are the disobedience myths such as those of Pandora and Eve, mythical women who, overcome by curiosity, disobeyed divine instructions and so let trouble loose upon all mankind.

Such simple explanations no longer explain, and such punitive gods are no longer credible. Yet the story of the dismissal from the Garden of Eden, and the sufferings that ensued, is a profound allegory. Leaving aside all attempt to justify the ways of God to man, what is perfectly clear is that if we are to grow in wisdom and understanding, to become persons, we cannot remain perpetually in Eden. In a life without conflict or burden, no growth can take place, no ability to distinguish between love and hate, good and evil, happiness and misery. The hero-God Prometheus realizes the hopelessness of this static condition, and so, to awaken man out of his passivity, he defies the ruling of Zeus, as Satan defied that of Jahveh, and steals from Heaven the 'fire' (symbol of new life) that will arouse him.

> 'Hear now the sorry tale
> Of mortal man. A thing of no avail
> He was, until a living mind I wrought
> Within him, and new mastery of thought.
> I cast no blame on man; I do but crave
> To show what love was in the gifts I gave.
> I tell you, sight they had but saw in vain;
> Hearing, but heard not ....
> .... till their eyes
> Were oped by me to see the stars that rise.'[1]

In this great myth, it is Prometheus himself who, as in the later story of Christ's 'Atonement', voluntarily takes upon himself appalling 'punishment' for trying to awaken man out of his sleep. In actual life, we must each decide for ourselves whether we will accept the burden of growth which increase of consciousness inevitably brings. The urge of evolution is towards such fuller growth and enlargement of consciousness; but because there is a

[1] I regret I have not been able to trace this quotation.

price to be paid, the Rise is sometimes misinterpreted as a Fall. In yet another great myth, Odin, the Father of the Gods, hung for nine days and nights over the void, and gave his right eye for the gift of wisdom, 'a sacrifice of my self unto my Self', that is to say a sacrifice of my lower self to achieve the higher possibilities available to me.

The Nativity

'As in Adam all die, even so in Christ shall all be made alive.' The birth of new life within us is symbolically expressed in the story of the Nativity. 'Unto us a child is born' whose name shall be Immanuel or God within us. Modern analytic psyschology finds that the image of a child in the dream indicates the beginning of new life in the patient. It suggests that the process of integration and individuation has reached a point which makes possible the awakening of life from a new centre which has come to birth within him. The 'lost soul' can now find his way forward from this new centre in the sure confidence that it will lead him to the Kingdom which is not 'golden walled afar' but in the deep well of his being, and from which he may take draughts of living water. The goal is not so much in the future as in the timeless moment of creative insight in the here and now. Therefore 'salvation' does not depend on believing the Bethlehem story literally, but on experiencing rebirth inwardly, for:

> 'Though Christ, a thousand times in Bethlehem be born,
> And not in thee, thy soul will be forlorn.
> The cross on Golgotha thou lookest to in vain
> Unless within thyself it be set up again.'[1]

Jesus himself made the criteria quite explicit: 'Ye must be born again' and: 'Except ye become as little children, ye shall in no wise enter the Kingdom of Heaven'. The seed of the new life lies deep hidden in the psyche as the grain of wheat lies hidden in the earth. Neither can grow and develop unless the soil is in good condition and unless the germ is fostered and nourished with whatever is necessary to its growth. The life will remain abortive unless it is made actual. The Boy of twelve, who had increased in wisdom and stature to the extent that he could discourse with the Rabbis of the Temple, was in process of making it actual.

[1] Whitfield, 'The Chambered Nautilus'.

The Baptism

The rite of baptism symbolizes the 'descent' of the Spirit into the *prima materia*, the elemental substance of life, as expressed in the words: 'And the Spirit of God moved upon the face of the waters'. The dove represents the gentle coming of the Spirit into the lives of those whose humility has prepared the way for it, so that the 'Voice' can be heard, bringing assurance of relatedness to the Whole. The pictorial language of 'Thou art my beloved son; this day have I begotten thee' points again to a Reality beyond the world of sense and indicates that the destiny of all men is to become united with it.

The report that at the moment of vision Jesus saw the heavens open and the Spirit descending like a dove towards him, is taken by the literalist as factual truth and dismissed by the sceptic as sheer imagination. There is however a third interpretation: the thing really happened, but in the soul of the Seer, not in the world of the senses. The place for miracles is in the inner world and true religion is a subjective experience rather than an historical fact.

The use of such figurative language to describe the indescribable is not unknown in our own day. A woman who recently took part in a religious healing ceremony in Mexico was asked by a friend, 'What was it like?' She replied, 'It was as if the windows of heaven opened'. In Chapter V we have referred to some of the men and women who, throughout history have experienced similar moments of exaltation, during which they became aware of the Reality which lies behind appearances. Many more of us would know the same experience but for the fact that, as Shakespeare said in reference to the music of the spheres, 'While this muddy vesture of decay doth grossly close us in we cannot hear it'. But it is our ego-centredness rather than our bodily vesture that shuts us off from the vision. 'Directly that by love we come up out of the water of earthly life, out of the small world of self-regarding impulses and thoughts which forms our horizon, we see, and see more clearly than the eye sees in the light of day, the heaven of spiritual Reality shining through the rent made in the curtain of custom and convention.'[1]

---

[1] W. F. Geike-Cobb, D.D., *The Path of the Soul*. St Ethelburga's Manuals. Printed at the Press of the Church of St. Ethelburga the Virgin, Bishopsgate, London, 1920, p. 68.

The Temptation
There is nothing symbolic about temptations as such since every Pilgrim towards the Beyond-that-is-Within is throughout his life assailed by them. One of the two protagonists in this story is symbolized as an external 'Devil' but actually the struggle is between the lower and higher forces within the nature of man, the former being necessary to the latter which could not otherwise develop the strength that comes through self-surmounting. The 'fasting' may be taken to symbolize a separation, not necessarily from food, but from a too great entanglement with the things of this world which might interfere with acquiring knowledge of the spiritual order. Hence the 'Wilderness' symbolizes the life apart, which is periodically necessary for learning more deeply of the laws of the spiritual order.

There was nothing obviously wrong in the impulse to 'command that these stones be made bread', to use inner power for the satisfaction of material needs, and in the feeding of the Five Thousand, Jesus is reported as having done so. His refusal of the suggestion on this occasion would appear to have been based on the need to stress that 'man doth not live by bread alone'. He cannot of course live without bread for, as Aristotle tersely said, before a man can live well, he must live. Jesus 'went about doing good' at the material level but he knew that his destiny was not to become a mere social or political reformer. His primary concern was to feed men with the bread of heaven, to awaken a higher spiritual consciousness in them. To neglect the spiritual for the material, to postpone the development of the inner life until order and comfort reign in the outer, is just as foolish as to do the opposite and take a Bible to people whose need is a loaf of bread. While we live in the body, a delicate balance has to be maintained between the material and the spiritual order. An infant in arms may wilt and die if given food without love, and those who ignore the things of the spirit in the midst of material plenty are on the road to similar disaster. In his reply to the first temptation Jesus was stressing 'the categorical imperative of the spiritual order', for he had come to know in his own experience that Spirit was the ultimate Reality.

The second testing of the quality and integrity of Jesus came in the form of a temptation to convince the masses of inner truth by an external demonstration of paranormal power. 'Cast thyself down'; that is to say, 'convince them through the evidence of their senses that there are other dimensions of being. That will be quicker than trying to make them understand; they are so slow of understanding.'

On the face of it, this was not an unreasonable suggestion, for it has to be admitted that we are woefully obtuse and that the life of senses is still more real to most of us than the life of the spirit. That is why a sign, something out of the ordinary, makes more impact on us than the miracles by which we are surrounded. 'An evil and adulterous generation seeketh after a sign' because it cannot recognize the divine in the familiar, cannot see that everything that is is a Logos—a word or expression of God—that everything which exists is holy and that the ordinary is as 'miraculous' as the extraordinary. We cannot be projected into such knowledge by a cheap spectacular 'gimmick'. We have to become capable of the deeper insight. 'Except I see I will not believe' was an admission of failure in Thomas to perceive truth save at the sensory level, failure to understand that the significance of Christ or of any saint is not the ability to perform 'miracles' but the power to see beyond the evidence of the senses. Many Christians tend to make more of the miracles which Jesus wrought than of the miracle which he himself was, in his capacity to perceive and enter into other dimensions of being.

The third testing 'Fall down and worship me' overlaps to some extent with the first. Its meaning would appear to be that it is the part of prudence to compromise and accept the standards of the world in order to win the world, to use wrong means in order to achieve right ends, to keep things going somehow in the vague hope that they will work out all right in the end. The reply: 'Thou shalt worship the Lord thy God and Him only shalt thou serve' means in effect that things won't work out and come right by themselves or by an automatic evolutionary process. There must be a metanoia or change of inner direction, a raising of the level of spiritual consciousness. This alone will bring about a change in ourselves and in the character of our relationships with each other. Such a change is man's deepest need; its realization depends on the union of the religious approach with the psychological.

The Transfiguration
An integration of all the psychic forces in man around his spiritual centre makes possible the flow of greater power through

him. When Blessed Thomas More came in from the garden where he had wrestled alone with the temptation to accede to King Henry's demands, his face was joyous as he announced, knowing what lay before him, 'I thank our Lord son Roper, the field is won'. And the clarification and integration Jesus brought about in himself after forty days of wrestling with the deepest problems of life made possible a still more vivid experience of cosmic awareness or contact with Supreme Reality. His three disciples saw him as 'transfigured'. Not unnaturally they wished to prolong the experience indefinitely, but life requires the vision of the hill-top to be tested in the plains and the market places, and the insight of the Seers must be woven into daily living. This is one meaning of incarnation.

The Crucifixion

The Cross, in its various forms, is a very ancient symbol which long preceded Christianity. It is to be found in the earliest records of man's thought about the mystery of life and of suffering. The ancient monuments of Egypt, Chaldea, India, China and Europe are all marked with the cross in some form, such as the Crux Ansata, the Crux Orata, the Tau, the Swastika. The emblem did not always represent suffering. The Crux Orata or cross of the praying arms was also the Chinese symbol for the life of plants and growing things, and is identical in form with the Greek letter psi ψ, which was used as an abbreviation for psyche, meaning alternatively Soul, spirit, mind, breath or life. When the cross was surrounded by a crescent or circle, as in the Ionic cross, it represented eternity. The swastika symbolized well-being and also the four elements of earth, air, fire and water.

In Christian times the cross was first used as a kind of monogram to denote the name and person of Jesus Christ and his teaching rather than his suffering, the teaching that the ego-centred self, the husk of the grain, must be transcended before new life can come to birth and that this means acceptance of the inevitable pains and disciplines incidental to growth; 'Freed must be the psyche from the pupa and pain is there to free it',[1] therefore it is necessary to 'take up one's cross' if one would be a follower of the Way. This truth was presented by Jesus, not as a personal and private philosophy but as a statement of fact about

[1] Edward Carpenter, op. cit.

life. It corresponds to the Buddha's 'Behold I show you suffering'; because suffering is inherent in life and is not to be regarded as simply something to be escaped from but as something to be learnt from, and, because God is in Man, to be transcended— hence the Cross surrounded by the Circle of Light. The Greeks expressed this truth in the brief statement 'pathemata mathemata': the things we suffer are the things that teach us.

Unfortunately as symbolism came to be replaced by realism, these inner meanings were lost, and the dying God was hung upon his cross as a mode of stimulus to arouse emotion in relation to the Person, rather than as a stimulus to search for deeper meaning. One such meaning of great interest has been expressed by Dr Cobb, namely that 'the Crucifixion of Christ is a special case of a universal process',[1] the process of the gradual penetration of matter by Spirit in order to give spirit form. The entry of spirit into form on the cross of matter is therefore a continuous process, a sort of Cosmic crucifixion which requires spirit eternally to compress itself into the limitations of form. Formlessness is not admirable in any art, least of all in the art of living, but form should be plastic to the uses of the spirit. 'The Cross, therefore, as a religious symbol denotes the world of form on which the pilgrim of Eternity must learn to stretch himself in order the better to perfect his individuation, and by limitation or concentration to fit himself to be a perfected cell in the body of the Heavenly Man.'[2] But the emphasis should be less on the pain (which when not resisted loses some of its sting) and more on the goal. It was, says Paul, for the joy that was set before him that Jesus was able to endure the cross and ignore the shame. Therefore the Greek letter ψ, meaning spirit or breath of life, would seem a more inclusive and satisfying symbol than the straight-armed cross representing the suffering on Calvary. The ψ includes this but transcends it, the uplifted arms reminding us of the fact (later symbolized in the Ascension) that Jesus had achieved a higher level of consciousness which enabled him to enter another dimension and so, to some extent at least, to go beyond the range of physical pain. This might well explain the strange words in the Acts of John: 'Thou hearest that I suffered, yet I suffered not. That I suffered not, yet did I suffer. I was pierced, yet was I not smitten. I was hanged, yet was I not hanged; that blood flowed

[1] Geikie Cobb, op. cit., p. 104.
[2] Ibid., op. cit., p. 110.

from Me, yet it flowed not. In a word, those things they say of
Me, I had not, and the things they say not, those I suffered.'[1]

The mystery is deep, but at least we can see that one aspect of
its teaching is that bodily form can be surpassed by spirit, things
'below' by things 'above'. In a sense it is true that Christ died and
suffered for all men because his heart was pierced by the pain of
the world which he felt in his own being. His death does not
however provide us with automatic salvation, for: 'It is also true
that every man born into this world must bear first the Cross of
the thief, and then the Cross of Christ in his own person.'[2]

The Resurrection

The Crucifixion and descent into Hades are followed by the rising
from death in a new 'body' (which nowadays might be described
as electronic) into a new order of consciousness, a new dimension
of being. Once again the question of religious import is not
whether this really happened to Jesus of Nazareth. The evidence
for Christ's appearances seem very strong, but in any case there
were people who had come to believe in immortality before the
birth of Christ. Aristotle believed that death is no evil but a good;
the Eleusinian mysteries taught the same, as have many deeply
religious poets and thinkers and teachers. The meaning of the
resurrection therefore does not lie in the historicity of the fact
itself, but in the ability to grasp the complementary relationship
of life and death; to realize that death has, hidden within it, the
promise of new life.

> 'For there is nothing lives but something dies,
> And there is nothing dies but something lives
>
> . . . .
> For they are twain yet one, and Death is Birth.'[3]

Ancient Egyptian wisdom claimed that our birth was also a kind
of death, that our Spirits have 'come down' to irradiate the dense
matter of an earthly body and thereby become enriched and
developed in a way otherwise impossible. The spirit becoming
enmeshed with the matter of earth may be envisaged as a flame
which must be tended and nourished until its work in the terres-

[1] The Acts of John, printed in *Texts and Studies*, Vol. V. Edited by
M. R. James, London.
[2] Geikie-Cobb, *op. cit.*, p. 112.
[3] Francis Thompson, 'Ode to the Setting Sun'.

trial body, and our work as individuals co-operant with it, is completed at this level of our being. The spirit then returns to its celestial source, enriched by its experience of suffering. According to this teaching there is no hell worse than the hell to be known here.

The Bhagavad-Gita also regards spirit as immortal:

'Never the spirit was born; the spirit shall cease to be never,
Never was time it was not; end and beginning are dreams.
Birthless and deathless and changeless remaineth the spirit forever;
Death hath not touched it at all, dead though the house of it seems.'

The Eucharist

The Christian feast of the Eucharist has many very old pagan antecedents. Common to all of them have been these two basic ideas: that death is necessary to new life and that communion between God and the worshipper is bestowed by eating the Body of the God.

In St John's Gospel, Jesus is quoted as saying: 'Except ye eat the flesh of the Son of man, and drink his blood, ye have no life in you'. This Gospel is considered by scholars to be an interpretation of rather than a verbatim report of Christ's teaching. Since that teaching was so often given in figurative language on which the hearer was intended to use his own insight and intelligence, we may take it that these reported words referred, not to a literal physical body as in pagan ceremonies, but to

'the holy bread
By which the soul of man is fed.'[1]

The great 'open secret' about symbolic 'Bread' is that it is present in all things, giving life to all and available to men everywhere according to their ability to receive and understand, and according to their willingness to 'die' to the lower in order that they may live to, and have communion with, the higher. In the language of evolutionary science, the matter might be expressed by saying that in man there exists every level of being from the dense, heavy 'matter' of flesh and bones controlled from the unconscious, to the complex convolutions of his brain which are controlled by mind and spirit. His destiny is to move forward, to be 'born' into the higher levels, not to remain stuck at the lower.

[1] John Masefield, 'The Everlasting Mercy'.

In making the ascent, the bread of Heaven, the life of the Spirit is 'closer than breathing':

> 'The drift of pinions, would we hearken,
> Beats at our own clay-shuttered doors.'[1]

The sacrament of Bread and Wine might be regarded as the outward and visible sign or symbol of this fact, this 'inward and spiritual grace' of the all-pervading 'Real Presence'.

[1] Francis Thompson, 'The Kingdom of God'.

CHAPTER VII

Paranormal Consciousness

There are more things in Heaven and Earth, Horatio,
Than are dreamt of in your philosophy.

Hamlet, Act I, Scene V

We have seen that among those who have achieved a high level of maturity there are some who have known, at least momentarily, a sublime experience of contact with a greater reality in which all sorrows vanish and all problems are transcended in an illumination of unspeakable joy and wonder.

In addition to this cosmic consciousness, there is another state of awareness which tells of a world beyond the range of our normal apprehension. This is known as paraconsciousness and it has no necessary connection with mystic union although it is sometimes confused with it. The Greek word $\pi\alpha\rho\alpha$ or para means beside, alongside or beyond. Paraconsciousness is that kind of awareness that, in some people, takes place alongside our ordinary stream of consciousness. It is not necessarily above the latter; it may be 'below'. It is a sort of 'No Man's Land' about which very little is as yet understood, and which has only recently been recognized as worthy of serious scientific attention.

The realm of the paranormal is a wide and varied one, concerned with such matters as psychodelics, spiritualism, telepathy, psychometry, clairvoyance, clairaudience, healing, fire-walking, automatic writing, etc. It is often supposed that a person gifted with special powers of apprehension in any of these spheres is spiritually superior to ordinary mortals. This is not necessarily the case. Psychical powers are like all powers and capacities, in themselves neutral and capable of being turned to good account or ill. To be the possessor of an unusual skill, whether in the sphere of telepathic receptivity, the detachment involved in fire-walking or the control involved in Zen archery, is not the same thing as being the possessor of intuitive insight and wisdom. Teresa's

77

saintliness had nothing to do with her capacity for levitation, which in fact she found more of a trial than a blessing.

But while it is necessary to make clear distinction between what is physical and what is spiritual, it is also true that the former *may* be a stepping stone to the latter; the paranormal experiences induced by taking minute proportions of such drugs as Lycergic Acid Diathymide, Mescalin or Psilocybin may, if taken under the right conditions, momentarily open the windows of heaven for us. Mexicans have long used peyote, the cactus from which Mescalin is derived, in their religious ceremonies, but the wisest among them have also known the necessity of making thorough and 'prayerful' preparation of mind and body, as for the taking of a sacrament. For if taken unworthily, it is the doors of hell rather than of heaven that may be opened. Aldous Huxley has been careful to stress that: 'Negative emotions—the fear which is the absence of confidence, the hatred, anger or malice which exclude love—are the guarantee that visionary experience, if and when it comes, shall be appalling'.[1]

There are no short-cuts into the Kingdom of Heaven; there is only the long, slow task of becoming more conscious, more integrated and dedicated personalities; and even when a momentary glimpse of 'Heaven' has been achieved, the vapours close again and the pathway has still to be trod, the battle to be fought. We clamour for immediate solutions and want to have quick and ready answers handed to us, to be 'told' in the same way that we can be told the latitude of Honolulu; but in the spiritual realm we can only have knowledge of what we have earned by our own efforts. A seemingly gratuitous visionary experience can help us along the Path, but only if wisely used. It will not do the work of self transcendence for us.

These truths apply in all branches of paranormal psychology, especially in Spiritualism. Belief in immortality would perhaps do more than anything else to bring man renewal of faith in life, but the agnostic who seeks a scientific verification for his faith will not to be able to find it by means of some simple psychical experiment. Moreover in this sphere, not only the charlatan and impostor but the merely foolish and immature have sometimes unwittingly brought harm to themselves and others. Stewart Edward White describes how a young woman, a sensitive and a

[1] Aldous Huxley, *Heaven and Hell*, London, Chatto & Windus, 1956, p. 51.

consciously sincere worker in the field of PSI,[1] came to him with a message purporting to be from his dead wife, a message which he at once recognized as phoney. In searching for the weakness which had made possible the entry of the destructive ideas through the medium of her automatic writing, Mr White asked: 'Tell me about your father; what were your relations with him when he was alive?' 'He always hated me from the time I was a baby', she said astoundingly. 'And how did you feel towards him?' 'Naturally I hated him back.' 'There's your soft spot. Hatred is one of the widest, perhaps the very widest door for the admission of destruction.'[2]

It is interesting to note that, until questioned, the woman had been unaware that her own childish hate had lived on. It is generally agreed that conscious hate, like love, acts as a boomerang, that:

> 'None ever hated in this world but came
> To very baseness of the foe he fought';

but that unconscious and unresolved post-mortal hate may do the same is an even more disturbing thought, giving a new force to Blake's words that:

> 'In Heaven, the only art of living
> Is forgetting and forgiving.'

The fact that psychodelics and spiritualistic research can be dangerous does not mean that they are wrong under all circumstances; it means that they should only be undertaken by people whose love and faith and integrity are of a high order, people with purity of motive, long patience and mature understanding. Such people were Stewart Edward White and his wife who together carried out research for many years both before and after her death.[3] A study of their findings conveys the assurance that no effort made in this life is ever wasted—in other words that the evolutionary process continues unbroken after death in those who have taken the responsibility of their own development and have at the same time a loving concern for their fellows. Mankind stands desperately in need of that assurance, but he wants to know that it is scientifically respectable, not merely a religious solace for grief. Is this kind of scientific research really valid?

[1] The term PSI refers to anything in the field of the paranormal.
[2] S. E. White, The Stars Still Shine, New York, E. P. Dutton, 1946, p. 173.
[3] S. E. White, The Unobstructed Universe, New York, E. P. Dutton, 1940.

One answer comes from Professor Broad, a scientist of high repute who himself once viewed with distaste the very thought of human survival, but later came to admit that 'a disembodied existence is not only conceivable, but need not be inconsistent with what we know of physics, physiology and psychology. It is both theoretically and practically possible.' For just as 'a piece of broadcast music may be said to exist in the form of modulation on the wave of a transmitting beam, whether or not there is a receiver to transform it into a pattern of sounds, so it may be that the "psi component" of a deceased human being exists in some equivalent manner'.[1] He also found that the famous Willet's scripts suggested something more than the mere persistence of a psi component. They made it 'very hard to resist the conviction that the mind of a certain person has survived the death of his body and is continuing to think and plan'.

The question of survival after death is closely related to the question of telepathy, since both are concerned with the possibility of communication taking place by some means other than through the senses. Extra Sensory Perception is a mystery, but so is ordinary Perception. We can trace the steps whereby light waves impinge on the retina, but we cannot understand how those waves come to be interpreted in the form of a complex visual percept of a table. This is the 'Great Gap' for which G. W. Fiske proffers what may sound just as fantastic a hypothesis as E.S.P. He suggests that 'each separate nerve-ending in its separate cell is like a tiny electric measuring instrument, a millivoltmeter registering the different potentials produced by the sensory stimuli, a million delicate meters each registering a varying response'. He asks: 'Is the brain comparable to the instrument room of some complex workshop? If so, who or what is the engineer in charge? Who or what scans the vast array of indicators and synthesizes their readings and so obtains knowledge of what is going on in the factory outside?'

Mystery surrounds us everywhere when we stop and look more deeply into what we habitually take for granted. That light waves impinging on the retina result in a *mental* event, a percept of great complexity, is every bit as inexplicable as telepathic communication. The latter is a relatively infrequent occurrence, perhaps because in the course of the evolution of consciousness we

[1] Quoted by Rosalind Heywood in *The Sixth Sense*, London, Chatto & Windus, 1959, p. 211.

have lost the capacity for this form of communication which was apparently available to the earlier and more open tribal consciousness. Primitive man felt himself to be in a state of fusion both with the outer world of trees, streams and animals and with the members of his own tribe,[1] but with the development of individual self-awareness this sense of close identity was lost. In order to become an individual, the ego was obliged slowly and painfully to free itself from the tribe and to take on responsibility for its own life. It is thought that the function of consciousness then became that of a funnel or reducing valve, an organ of selection limiting man's area of perception to what was of use to him and shutting out the rest.[2] Only when the brain is not functioning normally, when the efficiency of the cerebral reducing valve is lowered, as under the chemical action of drugs, do other 'para-normal' percepts slip through into the mind. Whence do these messages and influences come? And how do they penetrate our minds if these minds are entirely separate 'encapsulated entities'? Professors H. H. Price[3] and Gardner Murphy believe that they are not, but that two minds may 'overlap' by way of what has been variously called the 'psychic ether', the 'substratum', 'mind-at-large' or the 'field'. The last is analagous to the concept of the electro-magnetic field of physics. Nobody knows what such a field consists of, any more than they know what an electron is. The existence of a 'field' is a deduction. It cannot be seen or measured, but it can be proved to exist by its effects on a magnet brought within its range. Gardner Murphy's hypothesis is that we also are parts of an area of energy or energy 'field', and that telepathy takes place when a thought emerges from the mind of one individual and, perhaps in the form of an image, passes by means of the 'field' of 'psychic ether' across the threshold

[1] In *The Origins and History of Consciousness*, published for Bollingen Foundation by Pantheon Books, New York, 1954, p. 268, Erich Neumann writes: 'The sense of kinship felt by a human member of the totem for the totem animal and ancestor, and for all animals of that species, is carried to the point of identity. There is abundant evidence that such kinships are not just matters of belief, but matters of fact, that is psychological realities that sometimes result in telepathic hunting magic, etc.'

Freud, who was deeply interested in the occult, made the suggestion that telepathy may have been the original method by which human beings communicated with each other.

[2] This was the view put forward by Bergson in *The Origins and History of Consciousness*.

[3] Not to be confused with the notorious Harry Price.

of another mind. This 'ether of images' is 'not quite mind and not quite matter'. Its nature is as unknown to us as that of the electro-magnetic field, but if telepathy is a fact, some hypothesis is needed to explain its mode of functioning. Tentative hypothesis has never been frowned on in the scientific world; indeed it is only by the framing and testing of hypotheses, however seemingly foolish they may appear, that science itself can advance. In any case an open and imaginative mind is more likely to stumble on new discoveries than a closed and unadventurous one which shrinks from the possibility of finding anything unusual. Whitehead reminds us that 'the eighteenth century opened with the quiet confidence that at last nonsense had been got rid of . . . Today we are at the opposite pole of thought, and Heaven knows what seeming nonsense may not tomorrow be demonstrated truth'.[1] An example of this, and one which lends support to the theory of the electro-magnetic energy field, is the discovery of the aura by the conventional procedures of 'materialistic' science. The immediate response of the self-respecting rationalist to the claim that people have auras will again be: 'Nonsense', yet it is a fact that Dr Kilner, a London physician who was also an electrical scientist, has demonstrated that the aura is a detectable phenomenon. Eileen Garrett[2] quotes Dr Kilner as saying: 'Hardly one person in ten thousand is aware that he or she is enveloped by a haze intimately connected with the body, whether asleep or awake . . . which, though invisible under ordinary circumstances, can be seen when conditions are favourable . . . It may be stated at once that the writer does not make the slightest claim to clairvoyancy; nor is he an occultist; and he specially desires to impress upon his readers that his researches have been entirely physical and can be repeated by anyone who takes sufficient interest in the subject . . . There is no more charlatanism in the detection of the human aura by the means employed than in distinguishing microbes by the aid of the microscope.'[3]

Could it be then that our individual 'auras' are somehow related to that 'psychic ether' or electrical 'field', and that we are in fact all 'members one of another' in a more complete sense than St Paul realized? If so our responsibility for the thoughts and emotions we emit as well as for those we admit is tremendous, and

[1] A. N. Whitehead, *Science in the Modern World*, p. 161.
[2] Eileen Garrett, *Life is the Healer*, New York, Dorrance & Co., p. 120.
[3] W. J. Kilner, *The Human Atmosphere*, London, Kegan Paul, 1920.

the need for learning where and how to place our conscious attention is obvious. The following diagram roughly illustrates the hypothesis that interplay by a kind of osmosis can take place, not only between the varying levels of the individual mind, but

MIND-AT-LARGE OR PSYCHIC ETHER

The 'root hairs' represent the thoughts or images which flow back and forth between the different levels of the psyche and between the psyche and the 'Not-self'.

between our minds and the 'substratum' or 'mind-at-large' which is open to all and receives from all; that there are no impassable 'iron curtains' anywhere. Perhaps, as we work towards a more mature degree of spiritual consciousness, we shall recover *at a higher level* something of that sense of union and harmony with our Selves, with each other, and with our world, which was lost with the advance from the primitive 'we' of tribal consciousness to the evolution of separate individuality. The advance was inevitable and necessary to our further development, but the price of the transition has been so heavy that it is not surprising it should be referred to as the 'Fall'. We are still suffering the fearful growing pains of our immaturity. The cure lies neither in the retrograde step towards imposed uniformity on the one hand nor in anarchic isolationism on the other, but in further growth towards the mature 'we' of persons who recognize their responsibility both for self-transcendence and for service to our group, which is mankind.

Meanwhile modern man needs to reformulate his religion in a manner which, while not discarding any of the true values expressed in the religions of the past, is at the same time more adequately related to the scientific knowledge and the scientific imagination of the present. In science, as in religion and other spheres, are to be found both the rigidly fundamentalist minds which refuse to adventure, even in tentative hypothesis, beyond what can be proved,[1] and others able to imagine that 'there may be a leaping on to existence of new realms of experience; not an extrapolation of the present, but new in kind'.[2] The concept of other dimensions seems too difficult for the literalist to entertain, but to deny its possibility is unscientific in view of the fact that there are mathematicians who say that such possibility is endless and that a fifth dimension is already something they can apprehend. In his dialogue with Lucien Price, Professor Whitehead said : 'I see no reason to suppose that the air about us and the heavenly spaces over us may not be peopled by intelligences, or entities, or forms of life, as unintelligible to us as we are to the insects. In the scale of size, the difference between the insects and us is as nothing to that between us and the heavenly bodies; and —who knows—perhaps the nebulae are sentient entities and what we can see of them are their bodies. That is no more inconceivable than that there may be insects who have acute minds, though their outlook would be narrower than ours.

'My point is that we are part of an infinite series, and since the series is infinite, we had better take account of that fact, and admit into our thinking these infinite possibilities.'[3] What Science regards as feasible therefore depends not only upon the intellect

[1] An example of the closed mind was given by Professor Hebb of McGill University. When speaking of Rhine's work in extra-sensory perception, he admitted frankly : 'My own rejection of his view is—in the literal sense —prejudice'. Journal of Parapsychology, December 1952, Duke University Press.

[2] Professor Gardner Murphy.

[3] Price, Dialogues of A. N. Whitehead, p. 237.

but also upon the imaginative power of the scientist; and the agnostic seeking his way to faith in life will derive help only from open, comprehensive and creatively scientific minds. An Anglican priest[1] has described how, after the loss of his faith, new light eventually came to him through the chance reading of *Human Personality and its Survival of Bodily Death* by that scholarly and imaginative thinker, F. W. H. Myers, so that he was able to say: 'Through the gateway of this infant science, I have entered a new world'.

After reading, on her behalf, the address of Mrs Henry Sidgwick to the Society of Psychical Research, her brother, Earl Balfour, added these remarks of his own: 'Conclusive proof of survival is notoriously difficult to obtain. But the evidence may be such as to produce *belief*, even though it falls short of conclusive proof. I have Mrs Sidgwick's assurance . . . that upon the evidence before her, she herself is a film believer both in survival and in the reality of communication between the living and the dead.'

Mrs Sidgwick was a person of great wisdom and perceptivity and her scientific training makes it impossible not to take her witness seriously; yet for those who have arrived at faith in life through a study of its processes and participation with its Creative Spirit, confidence concerning the future is assured without the aid of either theological doctrine or psychical research.

One thing seems sure—that death makes no break in the continuity of our development and that we take with us only that degree of spiritual development we have attained here. It also seems sure that, whatever the nature of future existence, the battle between good and evil continues. The writings[2] of such men as Henry James, Charles Williams, Thomas Mann, Stewart Edward White and other thinkers of distinction, all support this view, and all give implicit warning that only the pure in heart and the well-integrated in personality structure, should presume to venture into the realm of the paranormal.

[1] Webling, *Something Beyond*, p. 20.
[2] In such books for example as: *The Turn of the Screw*, Henry James; *All Hallows E'en*, Charles Williams; *The Magic Mountain*, Thomas Mann; *The Stars Still Shine*, Stewart Edward White.

CHAPTER VIII

Cosmogenesis

The Kingdom is within you and it is also outside of you.

APOCRYPHAL SAYING OF JESUS

If there is an outer as well as an inner realm to reality, then our thinking, including our religious thinking, must take both into account and not ignore the one or the other; we must not seek to find aboslute truth in either alone, but rather in their relationship.

With regard to the inner, we have seen that the mystic experiences an ecstasy or cosmic consciousness which brings him a 'moment of truth' in which he 'sees' that the whole has living significance and 'knows' intuitively that all is well. We now ask whether the outer universe provides anything to substantiate this subjectively convincing experience. What sort of 'Kingdom' do we find in the outer realm?

In earlier times we found a reasonably secure and comprehensible little cosmos which we assumed had been specially created for our benefit; today we see ourselves spinning around on a tilted planet which in turn circles round a star on the edge of the Milky Way, the whole together travelling through space at unimaginable speed. No wonder Pascal said *'Ces grandes distances m'effrayent'*; and he lived three hundred years ago before the revelations of the radio telescope. The 'believer' may reply that mere vastness, space and speed diminish nothing of the beauty and order of the universe, of the magnificence of the starry heavens which fill us, as they filled Kant, with awe and wonder. True enough: but that is not, alas, the whole story. There is also chaos and cruelty and those terrible cataclysms curiously referred to as 'Acts of God'. And in addition to earthquake, hurricane, fire and flood, there are disease and intolerable pain and horror. Browning's cheerful optimism seems bitterly out of place under such circumstances

86

and we are obliged to ask: 'If "God's in His Heaven" what sort of a God is He?' We are confronted with the time-worn dilemma: 'If omnipotent, not good; if good, then not omnipotent'.

We shall never be able to resolve that antithesis by reasoned argument, so once again we must start at a different place. The astronomers are busy searching the heavens and some have wondered whether the God who cannot be found at the end of a syllogism may be found at the end of a telescope? In his Reith lectures, Professor Lovell said 'We hope that the radio telescope will probe the ultimate depths of time and space'. If it does, will that bring us any nearer to an answer? Astronomical facts and figures certainly stagger the imagination but so far they have produced no explanation of why the Universe exists, or why it is built as it is. The size and grandeur of the Milky Way stirs our sense of wonder, but has it any other significance? 'Man', says Nietzsche, 'can endure almost any how if he has a why to live for', but the astronomer seems no better equipped than anyone else to give us a why. Indeed in times past astronomers such as Bruno and Galileo have been held guilty of undermining rather than underpinning the security of man's faith, of taking away his why, deserving death in consequence. And later when the burnings stopped, theologians faced with the theory of entropy, resorted to subterfuge because the prospect of the heat-death of the world, however far off, would have shaken faith that life has meaning. So far therefore as astronomy is concerned it seems we are still left 'adrift and moorless on the pathways of the night'.

> 'We ask of the stars in motion
> If they have rumour of thee there?'[1]

and the answer is in the negative.

What of the other explorers of 'the outer', the students of the Natural Sciences? Here again, because of our innate conservatism and fear of change, new discoveries have often seemed at first more disturbing than supporting to faith. A hundred years ago, the publication of *The Origin of Species* came as a severe shock to those who believed they already knew exactly how and when, if not why, God had created the world. Old ladies are said to have prayed 'Lord grant that this evolution be not true; but if it is, give us grace to hush it up'. Samuel Butler accused Darwin of

[1] Francis Thompson, 'The Kingdom of God', from *Selected Poems of Francis Thompson*, p. 132.

having 'driven mind out of the Universe', and Nietzsche announced that God was dead.

Yet as we managed finally to adjust to the fact that our planet is not the centre of the Cosmos, so we have gradually accepted and assimilated the idea of Evolution and have begun to find in it grounds for faith rather than doubt. In the light of new knowledge our static and ego-centric notions are slowly loosened and surrendered until finally the external and anthropomorphic God of the primitive tribe or the little child, yields place to the concept of an all-pervading Spirit of life.

Now we are being required to stretch our minds yet again and to absorb a still more remarkable and 'incredible' concept than that proffered by Darwin, though it is but an expansion of his. The Report of the Darwinian Centennial Convocation held in Chicago in 1959 states that: 'The Conference frankly faced the fact that all aspects of reality are subject to evolution, from atoms and stars to human societies and values—indeed that *all reality is a single process of evolution*'.[1]

This is a stupendous assertion and one which at first seems too difficult for our comprehension, too improbable for our credence. It is one thing to accept that all life on the earth has evolved, but how can the entire universe itself be evolving?

The answer seems to be that the entire universe is alive and all its parts are related to each other, not as in a machine, as Newton supposed, but as in a living organism. 'The doctrine of evolution', says Whitehead, 'cries aloud for a conception of organism as fundamental for nature', and another scientist, J. S. Haldane,[2] says: 'Science must ultimately aim at interpreting the physical world of matter and energy in terms of the biological conception of organism. No lower claim than this will satisfy the ideals of biological investigation' or, we might add, of man's hunger for meaning.

This vision of the universe as a living organism is not altogether new. Throughout the ages it has been sensed by the intuitive insights of poets and philosophers. Among the ancients, Plato, the Stoics and the author of the book of Job, all believed the universe to be alive. Modern poets and mystics such as Shelley, Blake and Goethe and Jacob Boehme believed the same. More recently the philosopher, Dr. L. P. Jacks, wrote of the profound inspiration he

[1] My italics.
[2] Not to be confused with J. B. S. Haldane, his son.

received from listening to a lecture on the nebula Andromeda. In describing the effect that the inconceivable magnitude and stupendous grandeur of the picture made upon him, he asked himself: 'Is all that alive or dead? The moral law within, that I know is alive, more intensely alive than anything else that I know of. But is its life a mere accident, a trivial by-product of the universal industries, while all the rest is stone dead? Or is it part of a larger and longer life, which embraces the starry firmament above and links me in a spiritual unit with these amazing activities in the nebula of Andromeda? Of two things, one: either the whole is alive together, moral law and starry firmament dancing to the same immortal melody, or else the life that I have, moral law and all, is not worth very much. For myself, I cannot but believe that it is all alive, not as a vegetable is alive, but as I am alive myself. I think there is a soul in it just as there is a soul in me. I cannot think of all that as dead—while you and I and the rest of us on this insignificant planet are alive as solitary exceptions.'[1]

The concept of a *living* universe becomes less incredible the more deeply the matter is studied. For such study the reader is referred to *The Phenomenon of Man* by the paleontologist Père Teilhard de Chardin. In his introduction to this book, Sir Julian Huxley writes:

'Evolutionary fact and logic demand that minds should have evolved gradually as well as bodies and that accordingly mind-like (or mentoid) properties must be present throughout the universe. Thus . . . we must infer the presence of potential mind in all material systems, by backward extrapolation from the human phase to the biological, and from the biological to the inorganic.'[2]

This means that every minutest organism from the electron onwards, is the outer aspect of an inner essence, which becomes in man his conscious self. If this is so, if mind-like properties are present everywhere from atoms to cells and from cells to man, then mind has not been driven from the universe as Butler feared. On the contrary, its universal Presence would seem to provide the answer to our search for significance. We must agree with Edington that 'Something unknown is at work, doing we know not

[1] L. P. Jacks, A *Living Universe*, London, Hodder & Stoughton, 1928, pp. 39-40.
[2] Sir Julian Huxley, 'Introduction' to *The Phenomenon of Man*, Teilhard de Chardin, London, Collins, 1959, p. 16.

what'. But we can go still further. Among living scientists, there are those who find a creative trend in the evolutionary process. They not only claim that the entire universe is one stupendous process of becoming, but that 'all along the line through the ascending series of elements from hydrogen to iron and on to radio-active uranium, throughout the molecular world of chemists, from water and salts to the contractile fibres of a muscle, and in the realm of life from microbe to humming birds, as small units are joined together or as one item is added to another, the whole pattern changes as if you had shifted a kaleidoscope. And with these changes new qualities appear which may transform the old.'[1]

Such new qualities indicate that creativity is at work, for, continues the writer, 'If eyes and ears and brain and heart formed from the seemingly structureless basic living substance is not a case of creation, nothing is. It takes time to be sure, and is not a production of something from nothing, but beyond all cavil, with the expansion of a seed of life . . . new structure, new properties and new functions steadily emerge . . . Our common unawareness of it is irrelevant. The reality is there—creative development in every individual life and creative evolution through the course of ages.'[2]

This takes us beyond Edington to the hypothesis that 'Something *creative* is at work'; for we cannot suppose that this mighty sequence of events which from star-dust has produced creatures who can feel and think, love and aspire, is merely a matter of blind chance. To the concept that the universe is alive must now be added the thought that it is also the embodiment of spirit, or, as Gothe put it, 'the living garment of God'. In which case Samuel Butler and Nietzsche were both wrong. Evolution has not driven mind from the universe and 'God' is not dead. Earlier images and concepts of God are dead, or dying, and the Jehovah God who was said to have created the world at one stroke, in one week, from outside, now yields place to a 'God' or 'Soul of the universe' who creates not just a minor planet but a cosmos, not in a week but continuously and throughout all ages, not from outside but from within, and who moreover creates creatures who can themselves become creators, co-operative with 'Him'.

[1] N. J. Berrill, *You and the Universe*, New York, Dodd Mead, 1958, p. 94, *passim*.
[2] *Ibid.*, p. 106.

The Genesis account of creation was the work of an imaginative and poetic mind that had vision but no scientific knowledge on which to build his structure. Today, although we still know nothing of ultimate origins or ends and have no answer for the child who asks us 'Who made God?', we do know much more about *the process*. As time goes on new knowledge will be added, but meanwhile the Biblical story should be seen as one of many similar attempts among early tribes[1] at understanding how things began. The following account is in line with modern knowledge and is far more wonderful and inspiring than the old.

'Were it possible to witness the birth of a planet like ours at close range, even the most sophisticated intellect would find it difficult to believe that in the course of time there would emerge from that seething, billowing mass of incandescent gases with a temperature of fifty million degrees, a systematic order of evolution which would bring forth snow-capped mountains, tumbling streams, lush valleys and lakes and great oceans; that living organisms would take possession of the crumbled rock and turn it into fertile soil to nurture other living organisms; that ultimately humans would move through the forests and camp upon the plains. Humans, capable of knowing beauty and of experiencing love and awe and wonder; of developing art and evolving a science by which they could bring within the reach of their consciousness more and more of the stupendous creative power which brought their planet and themselves to birth. Humans, building cities and founding civilizations; building temples in honour of their unknown Creative Source . . . and calling Him by a multitude of different names.'[2]

[1] For examples of such similar attempts, see Sophia Fahs, *Beginnings of Earth and Sky*, Boston, Beacon Press, 1958.
[2] R. Alexander, M.D., *The Mind in Healing*, New York, Dutton, p. 65.

CHAPTER IX

Biogenesis and Noogenesis

*If the self-creation of novelty is the basic
wonder of the universe, the eliciting of
mind from the potentialities of the world
stuff is the basic wonder of life.*

SIR JULIAN HUXLEY[1]

Having glanced at some theories as to the nature and origin of the
cosmos, let us now come down to earth and ask a few questions
about the nature and origin of life on this planet.

From time to time we hear that scientists in their laboratories
are approaching a solution to the problem of life's origin, but if
the entire universe is one vast related whole and in a state of
continuous becoming, perhaps the problem is not so absolute as it
appears; perhaps there is no basic dichotomy between 'living' and
'dead'. Scientists themselves admit that it is not always easy to
say whether a thing is alive or not. A virus for example is only
alive when functioning as part of some other living system; it has
no independent life of its own.

It looks therefore as if some of our common distinctions are too
rigid and too superficial. Certainly the erstwhile clear-cut division
between mind and matter has had to undergo fundamental revi-
sion. Matter which was once defined as 'that which occupies space
and has weight' is now seen as a form of potential energy and
the body of man is seen as 'mentalized matter'.

An ancient Greek philosopher had the intuition that $\pi\alpha\nu\tau\alpha\ \rho\epsilon\iota$,
all things flow. Moreover in their movement they seem to overlap
and flow into each other, a difference in degree sometimes causing
a difference in kind. The water in the kettle is either boiling or it
is not, the difference being noticeable in the tea. Yet the boiling
water is only a little hotter than the not-yet-boiling. When it boils
there is no change of substance, but there is an important change

[1] *Religion without Revelation*, London, Parrish, 1957.

of condition. The same may be said of the difference between the organic and inorganic spheres. Teilhard de Chardin tells us that

'Everything in some extremely attenuated extension of itself has existed from the very first . . . In a sense we can no more fix an absolute zero in time (as was once supposed) for the advent of life than for that of any other experimental reality . . . Each new being has, and must have, a Cosmic Embryogenesis'.[1]

Indeed we cannot question this continuity when we reflect that all life has its origin in the star dust.

Yet the fact of continuity everywhere does not rule out the fact of new beginnings, or that apparent 'self-creation of novelty which is the basic wonder of the universe'. Changeovers, such as that from the chemical to the organic, clearly do take place. At a certain stage a new threshold is reached and

'the curve doubles back, the surface contracts to a point, the solid disintegrates, the liquid boils, the germ cell divides, intuition suddenly bursts on the piled-up facts . . . critical points have been reached, rungs on the ladder involving a change of state'.[2]

Exactly how the changeover takes place we do not know, but that there is no absolute break between one stage and the next becomes obvious when we realize that the cell, 'the basic granule of life', is not an object with no antecedents, but has its roots in the inorganic, in the nebulous gases from which all life has derived.

The encouraging thing for man's contemplation in this strange and paradoxical combination of continuity with originality and novelty is that what is true of the outer, of the biosphere and the elements, is also true of the inner or noosphere—the sphere of mind and spirit. For example, what is poetically called 'The Soul's Awakening', the breakthrough of new insight, is the resultant of all previous lesser awakenings and the 'critical point' could not have taken place without them. No past effort has been wasted. Even if it was made in the wrong context such as mistaken belief, growth has taken place.

If then everything that exists and everything that happens is on an unbroken evolutionary line between past, present and future, it is unnecessary to think in terms of absolute breaks between the organic and inorganic, or between animal and man.

[1] Teilhard de Chardin, op. cit., p. 78.
[2] Ibid.

As regards the latter, little observation is needed to discover that a 'Seeing-Eye' dog shows qualities superior to those of many a two-legged human; and a bird that will risk its life for its young needs no visit from the NSPCC. When we see the evolution of human consciousness as part of a vaster process, we shall not need such doctrines as that of a 'special creation' of man. Far more probable is the hypothesis that everything has been there in potentia from the start; that Creative Power has always been at work 'bringing order out of randomness, spirit out of matter, and personality out of neutral and impersonal stuff'.[1]

Unfortunately the habit of thinking in terms of evolution, development, and stages of growth is not yet very widely established. The average man prefers static and unalterable doctrines. Many also still find the idea of being descended from animals both degrading and contrary to religion. But if man's evolution is to move forward in the noosphere of mind and spirit, he must abandon inert ideas and static feeling and 'thinking'. For although there is some difference of opinion among scientists as to the mode of its operation, there is none concerning the fact of evolution itself. 'Evolution', says Sir Julian Huxley, 'in the sense of a process of genetic transformation of organisms, has been abundantly established as a fact.' He gives telling illustrations of the process. Having pointed out that many of the branches of the tree of life have become so excessively specialized as to be incapable of further improvement or transformation, it yet remains true that 'through this radiating fan of restricted improvements and blind-alley specializations, there runs a trend towards major advance; and this current of biological advance has continued through the two thousand million years of life's existence. It is marked by increase of over-all biological efficiency and by improvement in general plan of working. During its course, there has been an enormous rise in level of harmonious organization—think of a bird or a mammal as against a flat-worm or a jelly fish; in flexibility and the capacity for self-regulation; in psychological efficiency as shown in muscular contraction or rate of nervous conduction, or manifested in sheer strength or speed; in the range of awareness as seen in the evolution of sense organs—think of an eagle's eyes or an antelope's ears as against the complete blindness and deafness of a polyp or an amoeba; and in the intensity and

[1] Edmund W. Sinnott, *The Biology of the Spirit*, New York, Viking Press, p. 161.

complexity of mental processes such as knowing and perceiving, feeling and willing, learning and remembering, think of a dog or a monkey as against a sea-anemone or a snail.'[1]

Accepting then as we must the fact that this astonishing process of the evolution of life on our planet has really taken place during the past thousand million years or more, what are we to infer? Has it all happened in an entirely mechanical and inevitable manner, or does it indicate plan and purpose? The answer to this vital question varies according to the individual temperament and emotional constitution and the degree of insight of the scientist questioned. On the one hand, there are those like Dr Edmund Sinnott who tell us that 'Purpose is deeply rooted in protoplasm'.[2] This he claims can be seen in the fact that form and pattern are to be found everywhere, from crystals and snowflakes to more 'living' plants and animals. The pine tree, for example, 'possesses a bodily pattern to which it stubbornly adheres, maltreat it as you will. There is something within it which makes it a pine tree',[3] a self-regulative tendency causing it to develop according to the law of its own being. On the other hand, are those who like Dr G. G. Simpson hold that everything can be explained in terms of mechanical processes that 'Man is the result of a purposeless and materialistic process that did not have him in mind. He was not planned. He is a state of matter, a form of life, a sort of animal and a species of the order Primates . . . '[4] Dr Simpson calls his book *The Meaning of Evolution*, but it is difficult to see meaning in a purely mechanical and 'materialistic' process.

A recent attempt has been made to solve the problem of purpose by distinguishing between teleology and teleonomy respectively. Teleology is the doctrine which holds that developments are due to conscious purpose or design. Teleonomy by contrast denotes a non-purposeful process which yet works, like natural selection, so as to order or steer variation in a certain direction towards the end (telos) of better adjustment and survival. Thus special adaptations like protective coloration or long-term improvement for a way of life as in the evolution of horses, are said to be teleonomic,

[1] Sir Julian Huxley, *op. cit.*, pp. 215-16.
[2] Sinnott, *op. cit.*, p. 18.
[3] *Ibid.*
[4] George Gaylord Simpson, *The Meaning of Evolution*, New York, New American Library, 1951, p. 179.

but not dependent on any purpose, conscious or unconscious—as is implied by the use of the word teleological.

The distinction sounds subtle, but that a non-purposeful process should order and steer variation towards better adjustment is surely as strange a thing as that an 'Agent' or 'Deity' should be the directive force behind it all. As for the process steering life automatically towards survival, where does the mechanist place those who have chosen not to survive, those to whom spiritual values were more real than life? People like Socrates, Jesus, Edith Cavell and scores of others make nonsense of the 'Survival' theory, for to such as these the noosphere of mind and spirit is of greater importance than the biosphere. And to Simpson's assertion that the process is materialistic, one scientist replies:

'Rather I would say that if "dead" matter has reared up this curious landscape of fiddling crickets, song-sparrows and wondering men, it must be plain even to the most devoted materialist that the matter of which he speaks contains amazing, if not dreadful powers, and may not impossibly be, as Hardy has suggested, "but one mask of the many worn by the Great Face behind".'[1]

The opposition between teleology and teleonomy, between evolution by purposive direction or by mechanical Natural Selection is only to be resolved by thinking in terms of the different phases and types of evolution. To by-pass spiritual values which in man can act as a more powerful motive than the will to survive, is to ignore the problem. Sir Julian Huxley illumines it by making a distinction between biological evolution which is concerned with the natural selection and survival of the fittest, and cultural or mental evolution which is concerned with psycho-social selection. He explains that:

'Though natural selection is an ordering principle, it operates blindly; it pushes life onwards from behind, and brings about improvement automatically, without conscious purpose or any awareness of an aim. Psycho-social selection too acts as an ordering principle. But it pulls man onwards from in front. For it always involves some awareness of an aim, some element of true purpose. Throughout biological evolution the selective mechanism remained essentially unchanged. But in psycho-social evolution the selective mechanism itself evolves as well as its products. It is a goal-

[1] Loren Eiseley, *The Immense Journey*, London, Gollancz, 1958, pp. 49-50.

selecting mechanism, and the goals that it selects will change with the picture of the world and of human nature provided by man's increasing knowledge.'[1]

So life is being pushed from behind by the mechanical process of natural selection towards biological fitness, and being pulled from in front towards the realization and fulfilment of his highest psycho-social potentialities. We cannot know in any detail the nature of the 'pull' from in front, nor the nature of the destiny that awaits us in the far future, but two things are clear: we have our direction, and we have the responsibility for following that direction. We have entered into a new phase and a new kind of evolution, one peculiar to man, for man alone has the capacity to plan and purpose and choose, qualities hitherto absent in life. In short it is for man now to determine the nature of his future evolution. He may choose well and bring order out of chaos, or he may reject his powers and drift into further chaos and dark night. There is no absolute ethic to guide him, he must think things out for himself; and there is no irresistible force propelling him mechanically in the right direction.

It would seem that man is even now approaching one of Teilhard's 'critical points' when some climacteric change of great benefit to humanity could take place had we but the vision to foresee it and the strength to will it. Loren Eisely gives an inspiring account of such a change in biological evolution. Speaking of the transition of life from water to land, he tells us:

'It began as such things always begin—in the ooze of unnoticed swamps, in the darkness of eclipsed moons. It began with a strangled gasping for air. The pond was a place of reek and corruption, of foetid smells and oxygen-starved fish breathing through labouring gills . . . It was a place of low life. In it the human brain began . . . On the oily surface of the pond, from time to time, a snout thrust upward, took in air with a queer grunting inspiration, and swirled back to the bottom. The pond was doomed, the water foul, and the oxygen almost gone, but the creature would not die. It could breathe air direct through a little accessory lung, and it could walk . . . '[1]

Dr. Eiseley makes us feel that since 'a Devonian fish managed

---

[1] Sir Julian Huxley, *The Emergence of Darwinism*, University of Chicago Press, p. 20.

[2] Loren Eiseley, *op. cit.*, p. 50.

to end as a two-legged creature with a straw hat', anything might happen yet; that we ought not to let down that plucky ancestor but should try to accomplish our own advance and grow the spiritual lungs we need in order to be able to function in the new world we are trying to enter, and in order to be able to fulfil the destiny for which we have been created.

A small child once announced, 'I want to know all about myself from the time when I was a tiny speck'. He could have been given his answer in the bald terms of factual information or as a story that would arouse in him an abiding sense of wonder, causing him to rejoice in the marvel of the knowledge. For the story of the evolution of a child from a fertilized ovum is every bit as remarkable as is the story of the evolution of man from the microscopic amoeba. The latter has taken some thousand million years longer, but is no more wonderful than the development of the human embryo with its rapid multiplication of one cell into billions, and their gradual differentiation of structure to meet the needs of varying functions of the body. Surveying this process, Sir Charles Sherrington describes how, 'Some cells will have changed their stuff and become rigid bone, or harder still, the enamel of a tooth; some become fluid as water, so as to flow along tubes too fine for the eye to see. Some become clear as glass, some opaque as stone; some colourless, some red, some black. Some become factories of a furious chemistry, some become inert as death. Some become engines of mechanical pull, some scaffoldings of static support, some a system emitting electrical signs . . . '

It is indeed a thing to marvel at that an invisible speck of protoplasm, a cell whose diameter is not more than two-thousandths of an inch, should contain within itself all that is necessary for the creation of a full-grown human being, a being who has developed the power to study the nature of the cell and of the stars from which he has derived; a being with the intellectual capacity of an Einstein, the religious insight of a Boehme or the poetic power of a Shakespeare. No wonder Macneile Dixon should exclaim, 'Miracles? For my part I see miracles everywhere. I see nothing but works of magic. Miracles are not rare birds. They fly in flocks, they darken the air in their multitudes . . . Nature is not natural but supernatural, delighting in marvels, in confounding us with the astounding and impossible.'[1]

But for the mechanist, the fewer miracles the better. His hope

[1] Macneile Dixon, *The Human Situation*, London, Arnold, 1935-7, p. 430.

is that it will eventually be possible to explain all life in terms of chemistry and physics which have already accounted for so much that was once inscrutable and miraculous. The recent exciting discovery of the chemical constituent known as Deoxyribone-nucleic-acid or D.N.A. certainly looks like an impressive step in this direction. This astonishing chemical acts as if it were the 'brain' of the cell providing a kind of blueprint which determines the processes in the body of the cell. There is no further need of the 'agent' once postulated by the 'vitalists', still less of a Deity to give form and pattern to the flower and tree. To the poet's enquiry of the snowflake: 'What heart could have thought you?', the biochemist answers: 'Deoxyribone-nucleic-acid'; for this, it is claimed, is the organizing principle, the regulatory factory which guides development. But who or what guided the development of D.N.A.?

Something in man resists pat conclusions and feels that mystery remains. For how can a mere chemical have the imagination to frame the wondrous forms and processes of life? And even if the laboratory worker finally succeeds in creating life, will not life itself remain a mystery? 'What science will ever be able to reveal to man the origin, nature and character of that conscious power to will and to love which constitutes his life? It is certainly not our effort nor the effort of anyone around us, which set that current in motion . . . In the last resort, the profound life, the fontal life, the new-born life, escape our grasp entirely.'[1]

The confirmed pessimist claims that there is no sign or proof that man is even now evolving. Thinking in terms of historic time, he asks: 'In what way are we an improvement on the ancient Greeks? Can our threatened civilization even compare with theirs? Are we producing people like Plato or Pericles? Such questions are wrongly phrased because they are conceived in too short a perspective. The fact that — save for the abolition of slavery—we seem to have made no marked progress in the past two or three thousand years, is of negligible importance compared with the fact that in the past thousand million years odd, creatures which started as microscopic single-celled animals in the mud, have changed into men capable of thought and love and all the other spiritual qualities which dignify humanity.

Man is a very young species indeed and perhaps thirty or forty thousand years are needed to show any major evolutionary

[1] Teilhard de Chardin, Le Milieu Divin, London, Collins, 1957, p. 55.

change. But man has one immense advantage over the beetle in that instead of armouring himself in a coat of chitin, he has retained his suppleness and sensitivity and with it his power to change and develop further. He is not at the mercy of fixed instincts but is enquiring, flexible and open to life. Moreover, he is the only animal that provides for his young a long period of care during which they may learn how to learn and how to give and receive love. Their helplessness is their greatest asset.

It may well be therefore that unfinished man is only at the beginning of his evolutionary dominance, that as he is now, he is but 'the arrow pointing the way to the final unification of the world in terms of life'. Far from yielding to pessimism, the thoughtful, as Thomas Huxley said, 'will find in the lowly stock whence man has sprung, the best evidence of the splendour of his capacities; and will discern in his long progress through the past a reasonable ground for faith in his attainment of a nobler future'.

What form future evolution will take, 'it doth not yet appear'; but if it is true as Teilhard de Chardin says that 'Evolution is now gaining the psychic zones of the world', then it would seem that we should look for major changes in what he calls the noosphere rather than the biosphere, in the realm of mind and spirit rather than in the physical body—though there is no reason to suppose that beneficial bodily changes may not take place also. In any case some of those who have studied the matter most deeply find in evolution a trend towards more mind, towards an increase of knowledge out of ignorance, of sensitivity in place of blind cruelty, of the capacity to find significance in what once seemed meaningless. It is therefore impossible to believe that the psyche is mechanically determined and that man in his deepest and truest Self is nothing but the product of chemical processes. As one thinker has put it: 'That chemicals which are merely material should come to understand their own nature is a staggering proposition. Is it also a preposterous one?'[1]

Yes, if mind, thought and creativity are inherent in the 'stuff of the universe', it is preposterous. Man is more than chemistry. He is also more than intellect, and therefore in the search for truth he must use his whole self, his insight, imagination, sensitivity and capacity for mystic awareness. Ignoring any of these,

[1] J. Wood Krutch, The Great Chain of Life, Boston, Houghton Mifflin, 1956, p. 211.

his conclusions will inevitably be partial and imperfect; using them, he will be able to see farther than reason alone can take him. After the birth of her first baby, a young woman remarked with deep content: 'I feel I am part of the great stream of life'. An old man, dying in pain from a dread disease, said to those around: 'Make no mistake; life is wonderful'. Both these intuitive people, in what would generally be regarded as life's best and worst moments respectively, had come through their intuitive feelings, close to the heart of things, and had found deep joy and significance in the realization that they were part of the stupendous, incomprehensible stream of life that flowed through them and through all creation and made death, like birth, not something to be feared but a door into a new country.

Such experience provides solid ground for faith in life's process. It gives the individual that sense of relatedness to the Whole which the poet describes as the essence of true religion:

'Tis from the centre to thine utmost bound
　　To feel that thou hast found—
　　　That thou too art
From all to all eternity a part
　Of that which never was in speech expressed,
　The unresting Order which is more than rest.[1]

Scientists now tell us that the 'unresting Order' is continuously changing and evolving in all its parts. Therefore we, as part of it, must also evolve and having attained consciousness, must learn to trust the Process and give it our conscious and creative co-operation. Some four and a half billion years of stellar evolution, followed by one or two thousand million years of biogenesis, went into the making of a creature who can think and feel and aspire. We would do well to give this wondrous story more attention. As we do so it will become clear that our present and primary responsibility is to adventure as fearlessly into inner space as we have been doing, prematurely, into the outer. We can no longer rely for our salvation, either here or hereafter, on the atoning death of another; nor can we make any advance if we are content to be always 'other-directed' by authority. So, while discarding nothing that has validity in tradition, we must also perceive the truth of the Vedantist teaching that

[1] James Rhoades, 'O Soul of Mine', *Oxford Book of Mystical Verse*, Oxford University Press, p. 323.

No-one saves us but ourselves,
No-one can and no-one may.
Others only point the path,
We ourselves must walk the Way.

The Way is what Van der Post calls 'The Venture to the Interior'. The interior revealed by Freud is only part of the picture; the other and more important part is revealed by the mystics. Both parts must be known and integrated before we can understand Kierkegaard's saying that 'Knowledge of self is knowledge of God' or Christ's saying that 'The Kingdom of God is within'.

At the end of a lifetime's study and research, Professor A. N. Whitehead, whose comprehensive mind included both a powerful intellect and a deeply sensitive intuition, reached this conclusion: 'God is in the world, or nowhere, creating continually in us and around us. This creative principle is everywhere, in animate and so-called inanimate matter, in the ether, water, earth, human hearts. But the creation is a continuing process, and the process itself is the actuality since no sooner do you arrive than you start on a fresh journey.

'In so far as man partakes of this creative process, does he partake of the divine, of God, and that participation is his immortality, reducing the question of whether his individuality survives death of the body to the estate of an irrelevancy. His true destiny as co-creator in the universe is his dignity and his grandeur.' [1]

[1] Price, op. cit., p. 371.

CHAPTER X

The Challenge of Life

Let not him who seeketh cease until he findeth; and when he findeth he shall wonder; wondering he shall enter the kingdom; entering the kingdom he shall be at peace.

EXTRA-CANONICAL SAYING OF JESUS
Oxyrhynchus Papyrus

A speaker who had been lecturing on religion in the broad sense of the term was afterwards asked, 'What exactly do you believe?' He replied briefly, 'I believe in the Spirit'. As the attempt to define the word 'spirit' takes an entire column of even the *Concise Oxford Dictionary*, perhaps it may be more easily illustrated than defined.

None will deny that there are things in life of which the words holy, divine or spiritual may be aptly predicated. A great love, an overwhelming sense of wonder, the passion for truth, a vision of surpassing beauty, aspiration for wisdom and understanding, self-less service of others, courage to endure, humility to learn of the Way and to accept its disciplines, all these are things of the spirit which become real to us in proportion to our own level of spiritual maturity. They are not the monopoly of any particular religion but are the Highest Common Factor of all. They transcend all theologies and particularities of belief though many will feel that they at least point to the existence of 'the unknown God' or 'Holy Spirit' who 'beareth witness with our spirit'. In any case they must be felt to establish the fact that what we know of life is not all that there is to be known, but that there is a Beyond, which is also within.

Therefore the quest for meaning cannot end with a clear and final statement. Like all life, the life of the spirit is a process. Being but infinitesimal and rudimentary parts of that total

103

process, it would indeed be folly for us to expect neat and final answers about the meaning of the whole. We are not equipped to receive them. Such meaning or meanings as we can find will come to us through the furtherance of our own development and the realization of our relationship to the whole, not in a set of propositions to be believed. The demand life makes is not 'Believe and be saved', but 'have faith in the Process and co-operate with it'. The choice before us is not between 'being within the bosom of the church or outside it',[1] but between adopting a positive or a defeatist attitude to life, between awakening to ever wider horizons and interests or being content to drift indifferently on the sidelines; between resolving to 'stand or fall by the nobler hypothesis' that the process is meaningful, or throwing up the sponge because its meaning is not immediately obvious.

The challenge facing twentieth-century man in his terrible predicament has been powerfully expressed in the ringing words of a modern prophet:

'Take up again the individual adventure before it is too late . . . Walk out of your mind-made Kremlins before life stands still in you as it does in bees and ants which can only repeat themselves. Live your differences for love of the increasing wholeness it brings, and you will have adventure such as the world has never seen. . . . Live out your own nature fully and do not pile on the generations to come, who already have loads of their own heavy enough, the burden you shirked of unravelling your secret nature and letting out your imprisoned and unlived self.'[2]

The despair which assails us and saps our will when we are overcome by the horror and cruelty of life is best healed by remembering the true time scale in which we live. We too often think in terms of a few thousand years as a long time showing small progress. But to defeat defeatism it is necessary to take a very much longer historic perspective as does Professor James Harvey Robinson in his survey of Mind in the Making. He constructs a schema whereby 500,000 years (the lowest estimate of man's life on earth) is compressed into fifty, each year of that fifty to correspond to 10,000 years in the progress of the race. On such a condensed scale Robinson says

---

[1] Professor Corbitt, The Listener, BBC, 1959.
[2] L. Van der Post, Face by the Fire, London, Hogarth, 1953, p. 292.

'it would require forty-nine years to reach a point of intelligence which would enable our self-taught generation to give up their ancient and inveterate habits of wandering hunters and settle down here and there to till the ground, harvest their crops, domesticate animals and weave their rough garments. Six months later, or half through the fiftieth year, some of them, in a particularly favourable situation, would have invented writing and thus established a new and wonderful means of spreading and perpetuating civilization. Three months later another group would have carried literature, art, and philosophy to a high degree of refinement and set standards for the succeeding weeks. For two months our generation would have been living under the blessings of Christianity; the printing press would be but a fortnight old and they would not have had the steam engine for quite a week. For two or three days they would have been hastening about the globe in steam-ships and railroad trains, and only yesterday they would have come upon the magical possibilities of electricity. Within the last few hours they would have learned to sail in the air and beneath the waters, and have forthwith applied their newest discoveries to the prosecution of a magnificent war on the scale befitting their high ideals and new resources.

'This is not so strange, for only a week ago they were burning and burying alive those who differed from the ruling party in regard to salvation, eviscerating in public those who had new ideas of government, and hanging old women who were accused of traffic with the Devil. All of them had been no better than vagrant savages a year before. Their fuller knowledge was altogether too fresh to have gone very deep, and they had many institutions and many leaders dedicated to the perpetuation of outworn notions which might otherwise have disappeared.'[1]

But, it will be asked, what if there should be no generations to come? What if the power-lust or hatred of one maniac should, in a moment of de-control, bring about the destruction of the human race? What then? How is it possible to have faith in the face of such a horrifying possibility?

It is possible because there are those who have made 'the outward flight' and as a result of their venture, can say with the Hebrew poet, 'Therefore will we not fear though the earth be

[1] James Harvey Robinson, *The Mind in the Making*, New York, Harper, 1921; London, Cape, 1923, pp. 104-5.

removed, and though the mountains be carried into the midst of the sea'; or with the young English mystic:

> Though earth and man were gone,
> And suns and universes ceased to be,
> And Thou wert left alone,
> Every existence would exist in Thee.[1]

To the mystic the terminology is irrelevant, the experience is all. Whether he uses personal pronouns or geographical terms, he uses them as symbols with which to express the inexpressible. Vaughan's poem

> My soul there is a country
> Far beyond the stars[2]

is not referring to an astronomical area in space, but to the capacity of the soul to transcend the here and now and touch a Reality which lies behind and beyond all transitory forms.

A dying woman, confined and anguished by the bonds of the suffering flesh, also knew of a wondrous release into joy and freedom:

> Then dawns the Invisible; the Unseen its truth reveals;
> My outward sense is gone, my inward essence feels;
> Its wings are almost free—its home, its harbour found,
> Measuring the gulf, it stoops and dares the final bound.[3]

It is the belief of the author that there are indeed other phases and stages of being than the one of which we are normally aware, and that what the mystic experiences is in truth contact with a larger reality.

To equip ourselves through work and growth and service to enter into this Reality would appear to be the meaning and purpose of our existence here.

[1] Emily Brontë, Last Lines.
[2] Henry Vaughan, Poetical Works, 2 vols., ed. Chambers, London, Routledge, 1904; Selected Poetry and Prose, ed. Meynell, Nonesuch, 1924.
[3] Emily Brontë, The Prisoner.

Religious Education:
(a) Emotional and Social Aspects

And an old priest said, 'Speak to us of
Religion'. And he said:

Have I spoken to you this day of aught else?
Is not religion all deeds and all reflection, and
that which is neither deed nor reflection, but
a wonder and a surprise ever springing in the
soul, even while the hands hew the stone or
tend the loom?
Who can separate his faith from his actions,
or his belief from his occupations?
Who can spread his hours before him, saying,
this is for God and this for myself; This for my
soul and this other for my body?
All your hours are wings that beat through
space from self to self.
Your daily life is your temple and your
religion.[1]

KAHIL GIBRAIN, 'The Prophet'

Whitehead wrote that 'The vitality of religion is shown by the
way in which the religious spirit has survived the ordeal of
religious education.'[2] The following chapters, in which the illustrations are taken from actual experience, are offered as tentative
suggestions of the way in which greater flexibility and maturity
may be brought into religious life if children are encouraged to
build their religion on the basis of their own experiences rather
than on verbal indoctrination.

The test of all true education, be it labelled as religious or
secular, is whether it is furthering growth and development of
all aspects of man's being, but the more usual attitude is to

[1] New York, Knopf, 1934, p. 87.
[2] A. N. Whitehead, *The Aims of Education*, Penguin Books, 1938; New
York, Mentor Books, 1949, p. 50.

identify education with instruction and to regard religious education as a matter of teaching the young a system of doctrinal and
historical 'facts' which are not only to be regarded as unchange-
ably true, but belief in which is said to be necessary to our salvation. Moreover it is regarded as a matter of great importance that
this indoctrination should start as early as possible. The pro-
nouncement of the Spanish Founder of the Society of Jesus' 'Give
me a child until he is seven and I will let you have him for the
rest of his life' has been accepted as basic wisdom by the majority
of Christians, Protestant and Catholic alike. But if Ignatius
Loyola was referring to the value of early doctrinal instruction,
he was being over-confident. Voltaire, a star pupil of the Jesuits,
became the great iconoclast of his age, and many a less famous
child has also been alienated from all that is associated with
religion by being subjected to too much meaningless verbal
instruction, unrelated to the rest of his life.

There is another approach. Admittedly words have a valuable
and indispensable place in education, but the educator, as distinct
from the instructor, will not think primarily in terms of what the
child 'knows' verbally, or of the patter he can repeat by the age
of seven. He will think rather in terms of what will best serve
development. His concern will be to provide occasion for experiences through which the child can awaken to fuller awareness
of the deep religious truths which are non-verbal, non-
measurable and universal, truths of spiritual value which will
unfold according to our responsiveness to them. The following
examples illustrate what is meant by education of the emotional
life through feeling—experiences of wonder, mystery and joy.
The emotional life is of course never entirely separable from
thought and act; all are interdependent and of equal importance,
but one will receive greater emphasis than another at any particular moment. The first illustration of what is primarily emotional education comes from an American teacher of a group of
six-year-olds:

'They spent their Sunday morning at a chicken farm where they
saw an incubator filled with eggs, either about to hatch, or from
which the chicks had already broken through. The poultry man
took out an egg having already a "window" in the shell. Standing
in the circle of children, he gently broke the shell and as one child
said, "He borned the chicken". With absorbed attention the

children watched the chick struggle, finally take its first breath of air, and then squirm around until at last it got on its feet and flapped its wings and cried "cheep". When the door of the incubator was finally closed and the chick put safely back into its warm home, the children's emotional release took different forms. Some ran around the room, others clung to the teacher's hand, or began to talk. "I liked to see that chicken born." "It made me feel funny inside." "I didn't know it was like that." "Just think all these hundreds of eggs pecking away with chickens inside." "How does the chicken know how to peck all by itself?" "That was the first time it ever cheeped and we heard it." [1]

This is religious education at its best; the teacher herself was a sensitive person who had the wisdom to keep silent and let the facts speak. Had she started trying to explain or to draw a moral, she would have destroyed the atmosphere of wonder and mystery. She wanted the children to understand in and through their own experience that the 'Real Presence' is everywhere and that sometimes 'It' breaks through and wakens heart and mind to ecstasy as when the chicken emerges from the egg, the new life from the seed, or the dragon-fly from its case. All these with thousands of less obvious examples, should be experiences of the 'Blessed Sacrament', of the Word made flesh, for if the earth is the Lord's and the fullness thereof, it cannot be divided into two sections, sacred and profane. Buddha by way of a 'sermon' placed a flower in silence before his audience and Christ urged us to consider the lilies, for in the presence of such 'incarnation' all words are faint and, for those with eyes that see, no words can paint. Yet the mystic feels he must try to tell of his ecstasy, no matter how inadequate the words. Thus did Traherne in adult life write of his raptures in early childhood:

'All appeared new, and strange at first, inexpressibly rare and delightful and beautiful. I was a little stranger, which at my entrance into the world was saluted and surrounded with innumerable joys . . . The corn was orient and immortal wheat, which never should be reaped, nor was ever sown. I thought it had stood from everlasting to everlasting. The dust and stones of the street were as precious as gold; the gates were at first the end of the world. The green trees when I saw them first . . . transported and ravished me, their sweetness and unusual beauty made

---

[1] Beacon Press, Boston.

my heart to leap, and almost mad with ecstasy, they were such strange and wonderful things.'[1]

Later on when 'the shades of the prison house began to close' Traherne lost this sense of the wonder and glory of things but eventually came to realize that happiness could only be found in becoming once again as a little child. A girl who had lived much of her early life abroad did not see primroses until she was eleven. Then she wrote this:

> Like stars inside a green green sky,
> Like filmy drops of sunlight here you lie,
> Bathing in sunshine, washed in dew,
> No golden goblet held so fine a wine as you.

> 'Sheltered from stormy winds by tall kind trees,
> Opening your cups to welcome in the bees,
> No angry blast can your sweet peace destroy,
> Oh melting drops of sunlight . . . cups of joy.'

This is the experience which makes religion meaningful, the experience referred to by Jesus in the Oxyrhnchus Papyri, 'Wonder at the things before you, for wonder is the beginning of knowledge'. The Zen monk had caught the truth, and it caused him to exclaim, in the midst of his work,

'How wonderful; how miraculous this.[2]

> I draw water.
> I carry fuel.'

L. P. Jacks tells us that, 'Not long ago I met one of our great schoolmasters—a veteran in that high service. 'Where in your timetable do you teach religion?' I asked him. 'We teach it all day long,' he answered. 'We teach it in Arithmetic by accuracy. We teach it in language by learning to say what we mean—Yea, yea and nay, nay. We teach it in History, by humanity. We teach it in Geography, by breadth of mind. We teach it in the playground, by fair play. We teach it by kindness to animals, by courtesy to servants, by good manners to one another, and by truthfulness in all things. We teach it by showing the children that we, their elders, are their friends and not their enemies . . .

We teach them to build the church of Christ out of the actual

---

[1] Caroline F. E. Spurgeon, 'Centuries of Meditations', from *Mysticism in English Literature*, pp. 156-8.

[2] From 'Wash-day in a Zen Monastery'. *The Training of a Zen Buddhist Monk*. Kyoto: Eastern Buddhist Society.

relations in which they stand to their teachers and their school-fellows, because we believe that unless they learn to build it where they are they will not learn to build it afterwards anywhere else.' 'Do you talk to them about religion?' I asked. 'Not much,' he said, 'just enough to bring the whole to a point now and then.' Finally, he added: 'I do not want religion brought into this school from outside. What we have of it we grow ourselves.'[1]

This brings us to another fundamental aspect of religious education, one which needs a book to itself. It is that aspect which relates truths of value to personal development and to social relationships. If children are not getting first-hand experience and practice in the most difficult of all the arts—the art of living with oneself and with others—then they are not getting religious education, no matter how much verbal knowledge they acquire nor how many services they may attend. It has sometimes happened that 'Progressive' Education, in its anxiety to avoid the punitive and guilt-producing attitudes of the past, has tended to overlook 'the applied science of the inner life', and has believed that if children are allowed to develop freely in an atmosphere of sweet reasonableness, they will inevitably behave sanely and sensibly. This belief was more than a little naïve, for human nature is not that simple and a child whose emotional life has not become confused with guilty fears will freely admit to experiencing feelings of jealousy, greed, vindictiveness, the desire to feel superior and so on. These impulses are innate in man and must therefore be expected to manifest themselves at times in even the best conducted schools and families. But instead of being lumped together under the title of 'original sin', for which we must constantly plead God's forgiveness, what is needed is the cultivation of a scientific attitude towards human nature and human behaviour. The appalling history of this century should have awakened us to the fact that exploration of the self is the science of all sciences, and the art of living the chief of all the arts. The old theological concepts of sin, forgiveness, and redemption through the death of another, have proved inadequate. It is now necessary to undertake the responsibility for our own development. Quite young children, when they have been wisely handled, show themselves interested in the Becoming process and in discussing with reason and detachment how best to control negative feelings and anti-social behaviour.

[1] L. P. Jacks, op. cit., p. 52.

Finally, the universal problem, common to people of all ages, the problem of death, receives illumination when we think in terms of growth and development. The children, as they watched its emergence from the shell, were surprised that the chicken knew at once how to peck without being taught. It was explained that life is not passive either for the bird in the shell or the child in the womb; that both are providing themselves with what is going to be needed (eyes, ears, etc.) in the new world they are unconsciously preparing to enter.

Is 'preparation' the key word to our own lives also? More than two thousand years ago Heraclitus said that: 'Here we are as in an egg', and: 'There await men at death things they have neither looked for nor dreamt of'. Might it be that, if we consciously train ourselves by, in Aristotle's phrase, 'practising immortality' here, we shall find that death is not an end but is another major event like birth, setting us free to enter a new order of existence as unknown and unimaginable to our present powers of apprehension as is our world to the embryo in the womb?

Immortality makes sense only if we think in these terms, if we see death as a 'critical point' in the continuous process which goes on, in a new dimension, from the stage we have reached.

Religious Education:
(b) Intellectual Aspects

The intellectual aspect of religious education must needs be adapted to the intelligence of the child. There are those like the boy who said to his club leader, 'Don't ask me to think, Miss; it hurts my head, it does honest'; or like H. G. Wells' mother of whom he wrote that 'she went to a finishing school and at the age of nineteen she was finished. Ideas rattled round in her head like bullets in an empty container . . . ideas that were shaped thirty years ago.' And there are free and enquiring minds of the more intelligent who, very early in life, will start wrestling with questions of metaphysical import, such as 'Who made God?', 'How can God be in my house and Joan's house at the same time?'; 'Jesus is really better than God isn't He? because He came and did all the hard work'.

Rationalists would prefer not to expose their children to the idea of God, but that is an impossibility in our Western culture. Moreover, it may be that 'God' is a symbol word for one of Jung's archetypal images, arising in the deep unconscious in answer to a felt need. If this is so, it may be asked, why do people come to doubt His existence? Perhaps because the experiences of later life do not blend with the concept of God as an omnipotent loving Father. 'Don't talk to me about God caring', cried eleven-year-old Steve. 'If He cared for us the least bit, He would never have allowed us to be born to such terrible people.'[1] Childhood's God had failed him badly and no new concept had developed to replace that early anthropomorphic image. When this happens the danger is that loss of faith in the Personal Father image of God will be followed by loss of the moral values which have been related to and made dependent on Him. Once again therefore it is wiser to start at a different place, not with the Person of God but with the signs of God, since

[1] Elizabeth Myers, A Well Full of Leaves, London, Chapman & Hall, pp. 67-8.

'Whatever wakes my heart and mind
Thy presence is, my Lord.'[1]

Five-year-old Ellen says to her mother, 'The other night Daddy sang me a song and it had the word God in it a lot. I just don't know exactly what God means.'

'It isn't very easy to say what the word means, Ellen, but you know a lot already about the times people use the word "God".'

'What kind of times?' asked Ellen.

'Let's think for a minute. Why do you like to go woods-walking so much? And why do you like to go out and look up at the stars?'

'I just do,' said Ellen. 'I think the stars are as beautiful as the woods, too. They're different, but they're both beautiful.'

'And why do you like to visit brand new babies, like Susan? And why do you want me to tell you the story about the day Tabby Black died, every once in a while?'

'I don't know,' said Ellen. 'I just do.'

'Well,' said Mother, 'I think that maybe it's because a fresh new world and a sky full of stars and a brand new baby fill us with wonder. They make us think about being alive.'

'I like to think about Tabby Black,' said Ellen. 'I was sorry when he died.'

'For some people,' said her Mother, 'it's enough just to feel the wonder and to think. But other people write poems about how they feel, or paint pictures, or write songs. For some people it helps them in their wonderings if they use the word "God". Next time Daddy sings you one of those songs, see if you can understand what wonders they were feeling that made them sing. Then maybe you'll find out a little more about what the word God means.'[2]

This approach, even if it seems a little vague and difficult, at least a firm foundation to the idea of God as the Source of all that arouses wonder in us. It will therefore involve no later doubt and unlearning for the intelligent child.

The minds of young children are capable of receiving the germs of mature ideas and it is important for them to realize that these germs will grow and gradually unfold their meaning as understanding increases. Being already blessed with loving parents and a beautiful home environment, Ellen's happiness was not so

[1] George Macdonald.
[2] E. F. Hunter, *The Family Finds Out*, Boston, Beacon Press, 1951, p. 148.

dependent on the image of a 'heavenly Father' as is the case with less favoured children. If her good fortune continued, her religious life would gradually be built up step by step on the facts of personal experience rather than on the verbal facts presented to her at second hand.

A religion thus based and built will not break down in later life as religion based on orthodox instruction so often does when it meets the challenge of suffering, of science, or of other religious viewpoints than the one that has been given as the only truth. Children who can think for themselves are often extremely puzzled at the behaviour of the omnipotent, loving, heavenly Father-God who yet is capable of fierce anger over trifles,[1] and of meting out terrible punishments to those who disobey Him in any detail.[2] Unless therefore they are helped to arrive at a more mature concept of God, and to avoid a fetishistic attitude towards the Bible, they will discard the whole idea of religion, and relegate the Hebrew Scriptures—through which alone God is said to have spoken to man—to the realm of make-believe.

This is a pity, for these scriptures, in addition to containing passages of sublime beauty, are also of great interest when viewed anthropologically. They illustrate, as do similar scriptures of other primitive tribes, man's earliest attempts to explain the origin and purpose of the world as he saw it. They are also a record of the gradual transition of man's thoughts of God from that of concrete idols such as the Golden Calf, to more abstract concepts such as that of the prophet Micah.[3] As recently as the last century the poet Shelley was expelled from Oxford for his 'atheism', that is for expressing his disbelief in a God who was 'an almighty fiend, with a petty character and unlimited power, spiteful, cruel, jealous, vindictive, and physically violent'. A concept so awful that: 'The most villainous schoolmasters, the most tyrannical parents, fell far short in their attempts to imitate it'.[4]

[1] I Chronicles xiii, 9, 10. 'And the anger of the Lord was kindled against Uzza' (because he had put out his hand to steady the ark when the oxen stumbled).

[2] See I Samuel xvi, 3 for the terrible things which 'the Voice of the Lord' told Saul to do to the Amalekites.

[3] See Micah vi, 8. 'For what doth the Lord thy God require of thee but to do justly, and to love mercy, and to walk humbly . . . ' Such a God need not be envisaged in the form of a man. An Elan Vital, Life Force, or Categorical Imperative is sufficient.

[4] G. B. Shaw, *Back to Methuselah*, London, Constable, 1927, p. xxxvii of the Introduction.

Clearly therefore the question of import is not whether we believe in God but the nature of the God we believe in; not whether we think the Bible is inspired but how we interpret its inspiration. When it is presented to the child as a kind of talisman without discrimination, as God's unique Word to his unique people, sacred and equally valid in all detail, it becomes tedious, and of less interest than stories of Greek mythology,[1] or present day literature. Speaking of his schooldays, Joyce Cary wrote, 'We had our Bible lessons of course, but the religion which actually stayed with us, was something livelier, braver, keener than the church teaching; and much more real. A lecture from a boy's parent, a sailor, about chasing dhows in the Gulf, went to the bottom of our feelings in one flash.'

A religious education which is to 'take' must touch the depth of feeling and be related in a meaningful way to the child's own life, whereas a great deal of the Bible is incomprehensible and devoid of interest to both adult and child. Religious teachers are beginning to recognize these facts and those who conduct radio broadcast services to schools show commendable skill and imagination in relating their teaching to the understanding of their audience. But the important distinction between God and what people think about God is seldom made, and the Jewish predilection for direct speech in the telling of a story is seldom explained.[2] 'God did tempt Abraham, and said unto him . . . Take now thy son, thine only son Isaac whom thou lovest . . . and offer him for a burnt offering . . . ' is certainly more dramatic and vivid than 'In those days people thought God required them to sacrifice to him of their best, and Isaac was the best that Abraham had'. It is more vivid and exciting, but very much less accurate. Yet

[1] When consulted by Professor Jowett of Oxford about the compilation of a Children's Bible, Florence Nightingale sent with her list of suitable stories this comment: 'There are some things in Homer we might better call "Holy Writ", many, many in Sophocles and Aeschylus. The stories about Andromache and Antigone are worth all the women in the Old Testament put together. The story of Achilles and his horses is far more fit for children than that of Balaam and his ass.'

[2] A seven-year-old girl of unusual insight suddenly exclaimed in class: 'Oh I see now; God didn't really want Abraham to kill his son; Abraham only thought He did'. She was perhaps the only one of the group to perceive the implication of the difference—that one could not treat the Bible as literal truth.

when such passages are read in church, they are left as they stand without any attempt at elucidation.

For the sake of brevity, the following illustrative discussions have been compressed into one session. In actual fact they took place at odd times over an entire year, mainly with two different classes ranging in age from six to eight and eight to ten respectively, in a private school which gave no official Scripture teaching as such, but which, while conducting school prayers each morning and giving tacit approval to Church and Sunday School, also gave complete freedom to the teacher.

I had given the older children a short course of lessons on Evolution and taught them the meaning of symbolic and figurative speech as a background for their general understanding.

It will be obvious that the greater part of the discussion was carried on, as is always the case, by a few of the more reflective and/or the more articulate children. It will also be obvious that the dialogue went much less smoothly in the classroom than as here described. My main purpose was to encourage free thought and expression and widen religious horizons, and at the same time to avoid clashing too disturbingly with whatever was being taught in the various churches which, willingly or unwillingly, most of them attended.

There had been a disaster one morning in the playground. The children had found a wounded bird. They placed it lovingly in a basket of leaves which they put on a high wall for safety. Here it was found by the neighbour's cat, and a shudder of consternation went through the classroom. Winifred had evidently been deeply disturbed about the matter, for in the course of a later (Arithmetic) lesson she asked with apparent irrelevance: 'Why does God do it like that?'

Teacher: 'Like what, Winifred?'

Winifred: 'Why does He let the cat eat the poor little bird?'

Jill: 'Yes, and let the bird eat the poor little caterpillar?'

T: 'I don't know. No one in the world can really answer your question: no one is wise enough. I am glad you asked it because that shows you are thinking for yourself, but one of the most important things to realize is that there is a great deal in life which we cannot understand; much of it very sad, like the fate of this bird.'

Jim: 'But you always tell us to try and understand.'

T: 'I still do, but we must also face the fact that at our lowly stage of development, there is a great deal we cannot understand and must simply accept. Anyway I can tell you for your comfort that I don't think the bird felt anything at all.'[1] I explained about its less highly developed nervous system, but the children made it clear that this was a far from satisfactory answer.

Anne: 'I don't see it; Jesus said not a sparrow would fall to the ground without God knowing about it. If He looks after everything and can do what He likes, why did He let this happen?'

Martha: 'Maybe God can't do what He likes.'

Tom: 'Maybe He makes mistakes like we do, and wants us to help Him.'

T: 'Perhaps that is part of the answer—that He needs our help. Many people have believed that God depends on us as we do on Him. If that's true, then it means we have a tremendous responsibility to do all that we can to help to bring more kindness and less cruelty into the world. We don't know anything about God really, but we do know that we can grow a little wiser, and when we are wise enough we shall see things differently. We have to keep remembering that we aren't very highly developed creatures ourselves yet. We are rather like the caterpillar who can't see anything of the world beyond his cabbage leaf and so thinks that is all there is. Perhaps some day when we have cracked our shells or worked out of our cocoons, we shall understand why all these tragic things happen, but meanwhile we must just go on from where we are.'

Martha: 'Could God really be growing too, just as we do?'

T: 'Some people think so.'

Alison: (aged six, in a casual aside.) 'My mummy doesn't believe any of this. She doesn't believe in God and she doesn't believe in Jesus.'

Helen: (shocked) ' "Doesn't believe in God"? She *ought* to.'

---

[1] Later I told them the story of Livingstone who said he had felt nothing when he was being mauled by a lion.

T: 'We won't tell other people what they ought to believe, Helen. That's one of the things I'm quite sure we ought not to do. It's not our business. Besides, we don't know *which* God Cicely's mother doesn't believe in. Perhaps I don't believe in Him either. It isn't the word 'God' that matters, but what you mean when you use it. What do you mean?'

(Helen didn't know, but seven-year-old Jean said, with pride in her superior wisdom:)

Jean: 'I used to think when I was little, that God was a person, a sort of big Man, sitting on a throne up in the sky.'

T: 'And what do you think now?'

Jean: 'That He's a spirit.'

T: 'Which means?'

Tom: 'Something you can't see.'

T: 'Can a thing be real if you can't see it? Try to think of of something which you are sure exists, but which cannot be seen.'

Helen: 'Love'.

T: 'Yes, you can see people doing loving deeds, but you can't see love. St John described God in the one word: 'love'.[1] He also said that anyone who loved was 'of God'; and your mother loves you, Alison?'

Alison: 'Of course she does.'

T: 'Well, then you could say she is "of God" or "in God".'

Rex: 'How could anybody be in God?'

T: 'Listen to this short fable and see if it helps you towards an answer.

' "Don't you know you're in great danger, little fishes?" croaked the frog.
"No", cried the fishes, much frightened.
"Don't you know fishes can't live without water?" teased the cruel frog. "You'd better find some water quickly, or you'll die."
The little fishes ran to their mother in great distress.
"Oh, Mother, Mother. The frog says if we don't find some water quickly we'll die. Mother, what's water?"
"I don't know," confessed the Mother Fish . . . "I never heard anything about water. Let's go and ask the otter."

[1] John iv, 8.

"Water, my dears?" laughed the otter. "Why, you live in water. That's what you breathe." '

I reminded the class of another writer who said, "He is not far from each one of us; for in Him we live and move and have our being".[1]

Rex: 'You mean, we're like the fishes?'
Ben: 'And God is the water?'
T: 'Something like that. Not exactly like it of course; it's figurative language, but it helps you to think of God in a different way from the old way as a strange sort of Man in the Sky. Instead of water, you could think of Him as the living Being of everything, the spiritual essence that gives life to everything, like the sap that pervades and gives life to all parts of the tree. You sometimes sing that hymn in church:

"To all life thou givest—to both great and small;
In all life thou livest, the true life of all." '

James: (bringing things down to earth.) 'If God is everywhere, is He in my pencil box?' (Laughter.)
T: 'If He is in everything, He must be in your pencil box, at some level of His being.'

This was introducing a new concept, not easy to explain. Martha interrupted with: 'My Vicar says Jesus is God'.

T: 'Yes, we might say Jesus is God at a very high level of being, because he cared only about the things of God, that is about loving-kindness and beauty and courage; and the pencil box is God at a very low level of being, for it isn't even conscious.'
James: 'It isn't even alive.'
T: 'Actually I think it is, in a very strange and lowly kind of way. I think everything is alive in some way because it is part of the Whole Universe and so shares in the life of the whole, just as the millions of cells in you share the life of your body. I think the Universe is alive, and everything in it is related and so must share in the life of the whole.
Jill: 'My Mummy says she goes to the early Service to get the Jesus-life in her.'

[1] Acts xvii, 28.

T :   'Most Christians like to do that: they feel He had so
           much of this spirit-life in Him that they like to remem-
           ber Him in this way, as he is said to have suggested
           they should. Of course the bread is only a *symbol* of
           the spirit-life or Christ-life. Everybody has to win the
           life for themselves and how well we win it depends on
           how hard we are prepared to work on ourselves to
           improve the quality of our receiving sets, that is, our-
           selves. And by the way, there is something else which
           is real but invisible, our selves.'
Robert :   'Yes, and I thought of the electricity waves in the air.'
Tom :   'And sound waves and light waves.'
T :   'Perhaps, some day, we will discover thought waves
           too.'

I gave them an illustration, sent me by a friend in America, of
how to improve one's 'receiving set':

'We had been experimenting with different kinds of light. The
children had made rainbows with glass prisms, and soap-bubbles,
and tallow candles, and they had looked at the moon through the
College telescope. Then they looked at the stars at night and
afterwards made this little poem:

> 'Why is the sky at night like a Friends' Meeting?
>   There are no words;
>   There is silence all around us;
>   Yet we are getting a message.'

I explained to my class the nature and purpose of a Friends'
Meeting, how Friends come together to try and experience in
silence the Presence of God which they believe is within us and
around us all the time, waiting our awakening to it. I told them
the story of the Fierce Feathers[1] and how the Red Indians, who
came intending to destroy a white settlement, laid down their
spears, when they saw the silent meeting, saying with surprise,
'Great Spirit inside Indian too': and they quietly sat down and
joined in the silent worship.
Carol :   'I like that name for God: "The Great Spirit".'
T :   'So do I. But you know it doesn't really matter what
           name you use so long as you get the message.'
Cecil :   'My father lived in India and he says they have lots of
           names for God there.'

[1] L. Violet Hodgkin, *Fierce Feathers*, Harrogate, Robert Davis, 1905.

T: 'If we collected all the names that have ever been invented for God, we should have an enormous number.'

We thought of some and between us we produced Deus, Dieu, Gott, Allah, Vishnu, etc. I told them of the Hindu Brahman, the great Unknown 'God behind the gods', and of Atman, the god within us; of the ancient Egyptians with their Holy Family, Osiris and Isis and their son Horus; and of the Persians who thought of God as Light, Ahura Mazda (the word that used to be on our electric light bulbs). Somebody mentioned Odin and Thor, the gods of the Norsemen and those of the Greeks. Mary felt dubious about including these since the Norsemen were 'heathen' and their gods were not real, but only what they imagined.

T: 'That is true about the gods of many people, Mary. The early Jews called their god Jehovah or Jahveh and they imagined some pretty strange things about him.

Mary: (shocked and puzzled). 'But he's the one true God. The Bible says so.'

T: 'Yes, but as with the pencil box, you now have to learn to see the Bible at different levels. It is not one book but a great many books expressing different levels of understanding. At the earliest levels, God was pictured as a very ferocious creature who sent bears out of the wood to devour naughty children; who required people to offer Him blood sacrifices, and who inflicted appalling punishments on those who didn't do exactly what He said, as if He was a terrifying vengeful Judge. Much later came wise prophets and teachers like Micah and Jesus who told people their image of God was a wrong one, that God didn't want their burnt offerings; that He was loving and forgiving, not vengeful and punitive. As most people need an image of God, Jesus gave them the image of Him as a loving Father to replace the old image of a fierce Judge. For most people it seems easier to think of God that way, as a Father, than as the Spirit of Life. Christians generally think of Him as Father now. Anyway, whatever name you like to use, remember the name is only a symbol for the Spirit of life of which we know and understand so little, but from Which, or from Whom, we can receive messages like those Quaker children.'

Tom:	'D'you mean we could make up our own name for Him?'
T:	'Yes, of course you could, only the name "God" is the one we all use in the West, so it seems more convenient to keep to it.'
Jane:	'You know, when I'm told I ought to love God, I feel terrible because I don't and I can't; my mind's a blank if I try to think of Him.'
T:	'You needn't feel guilty about it, Jane. Lots of children feel the same way; I used to myself. You can't love a "Person" you know nothing about and can't imagine, but you can and do love what are called the things of God, the 'messages' as we might call them: it's the loving that matters. I once read of a girl who loved the clover-flower and felt it brought her a message, though she could not put it into words. I have always felt the first snowdrop is like a wonderful message.'
Jane:	'I think that's what I feel when my baby brother smiles at me.'

Others began to contribute their 'messages'; their first sight of the sea in summer; the smell of seaweed; the red holly berries, walking barefoot on the grass, and Daddy saying 'My dearest' to Mummy, etc.

T:	'Well, these are your pictures or messages. There are plenty of things to love and you could if you like think of God as the Source of all good things. You can't imagine what the Source is like, so don't try to picture God Himself, but be content with the messages that come through. You can think of God the way Jesus suggested, as a Loving Father, but remember that is only a symbol, so if it bothers you, do like the Buddhists, leave God out of the picture, and just concentrate on the things we can know and love, and try to make more of them in the world.'
Sam:	'You've left out what you told us about thinking of God as the Life of everything in the world.'
T:	'So I have, and that's the way that I like best to think myself; and the line I like which expresses it, says:

"I am the stream of life which flows through thee."

You see, it's as if we are in the stream, and its life

flows through us, just as a cell might say, "I am in the body of this boy Sam and he is in me because his life flows through me and gives life to me". There is a prayer sometimes used in church which says the same thing in another way. It speaks of God as "the Light of the minds which know Thee; the joy of the hearts that love Thee, and the strength of the wills that serve Thee". That is what Jesus meant when he said the Kingdom of God is within us. It is what Blake meant in his poem:

> "Where mercy, love and pity dwell,
> There God is dwelling too"[1]

and what another poet meant when he said:

> "This thing is God:
> To be man with thy might."[2]

Hilda:	'You mean God is really anything that is good?'
Jill:	'The two words are nearly the same except for an "o".'
Tom:	'So are evil and devil nearly the same.'
T:	'Yes, taking an "o" and putting in a "d" makes them into "Persons". That is what we mean by the word "personify". You see Carol, you need not worry over not being able to imagine what God is like or to feel love for "Him", because there is always goodness and beauty to love, that is if you care about goodness and beauty.'
Carol:	(fervently.) 'Oh I do.'
T:	'I think most people do really, unless something has gone badly wrong with them. But of course different people have different ideas as to what is good.'
Tom:	'Hitler didn't.'
T:	'No, but I believe he was a case where something had gone badly wrong in his early life and so he learned to hate instead of love.'
Fred:	'What does that mean "to be man with thy might"?'
T:	'It means doing the best you can, like when you sweep the path so vigorously, Fred. It's a bit like that line

[1] Poem by William Blake, 1757-1827. 'To Mercy, Pity, Peace and Love'.
[2] Swinburne, Songs Before Sunrise, 'Hertha', Stanza 15, London, Heinemann, 1871.

in the American hymn I taught you[1] : "Thou hast put an upward reach into the heart of man".

Sybil: 'Does that mean growing upwards like the plants?'

T: 'Yes, only we have to grow in different ways, in more than one way. The bulbs and seeds grope their way through the dark earth towards the light of the sun, but even though there seems to be something directing their growth, they do not have anything that could be called conscious mind. They have an "upward reach" but only at the physical level. We could say that they have in them, in a lowly form, *that* from which conscious mind develops. Only they do not have to work at helping their minds grow as we do.'

Molly: 'We can't make anything as beautiful as the flowers.'

T: 'Isn't that astonishing? Although man has achieved consciousness and can make machinery and books and houses, he cannot make a flower.'

Dick: 'So he's not so wonderful as he likes to think?'

T: 'Well, he is still very ignorant and far from being as wonderful as he may yet become. If you look at the time chart[1] again, you will see why. Remember that this chart only goes back to Paleolithic times so it doesn't even cover man's odd million or half-million years on the earth, whereas life itself has been here for one or two thousand million years. So although we may think ourselves very advanced creatures, we really only arrived as it were a few weeks ago and have a long journey and an exciting journey before us.'

Jane: 'I think I see what you mean about the caterpillar.'

Tom: 'Yes, how can the caterpillar tell what the gardener is doing?'

T: 'And how can he possibly imagine what the future holds for him and picture himself as a butterfly?'

Tom: 'He's much too stupid for that.'

T: 'We are sometimes just as stupid when we think we have arrived at the last stage of our journey and know

---

[1] Hymn 271, in *We Sing of Life*, Boston, Beacon Press, 1955.

[2] This was a line of time which went horizontally round the wells of the classroom representing the time of civilized man in relation to neolithic and paleolithic man.

all the answers to life. Our evolution has a long way to go yet.'

Martha :   'I wonder what our next stage will be?'
(Chorus from boys.) 'Space men.'

A girl :   'No, better men.'

T :   'I suppose there isn't any reason why there shouldn't be both—space men and better men. But as we have not yet learnt how to live together without fighting each other on this planet, and we shall not do so until we become better men, that is certainly more important than space travel.'

Ted :   'Gabriel[1] said the worst thing we could do is lose our power to feel.'

T :   'Why would that matter so much?'

Jane :   'Because if we stopped feeling we would stop thinking and growing.'

T :   'Yes, it's this growing we have to concentrate on. Bodies stop growing but our minds can grow as long as we live, and if we see to it that they do, we shall be helping the great life-process forward.'

[1] The earlier lessons on evolution were based on Gerald Heard, *Gabriel and the Creatures*, New York, Harper, 1952.
